# THE BEST OF JEWEL

## CONTENTS

Cover photo by Jennifer Graylock - Retna Ltd.

Music transcriptions by Steve Gorenberg

ISBN 0-634-06716-8

HAL•LEONARD®
CORPORATION
7777 W. BLUEMOUND RD. P.O. BOX 13819 MILWAUKEE, WI 53213

Visit Hal Leonard Online at
**www.halleonard.com**

from *Pieces of You*

# Angel Standing By

### Words and Music by Jewel Kilcher

Open D tuning, down 1/2 step:
(low to high) Db-Ab-Db-F-Ab-Db

**Intro**
Moderately ♩ = 64

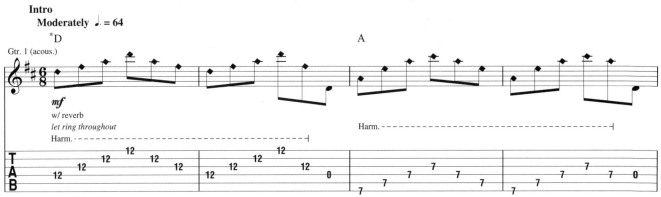

*Chord symbols reflect implied harmony.

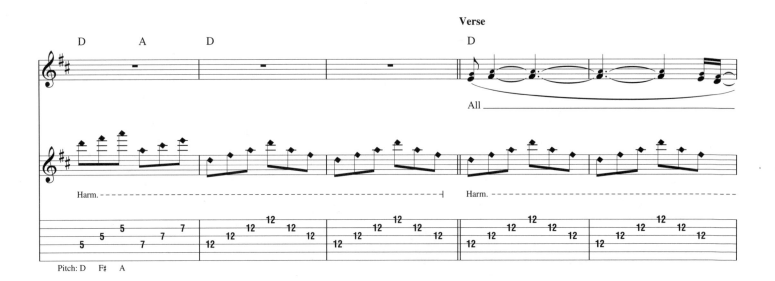

Pitch: D  F♯  A

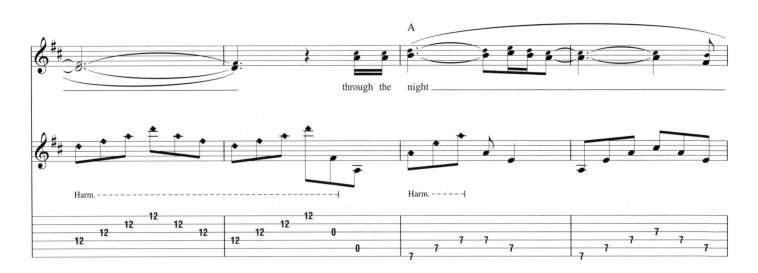

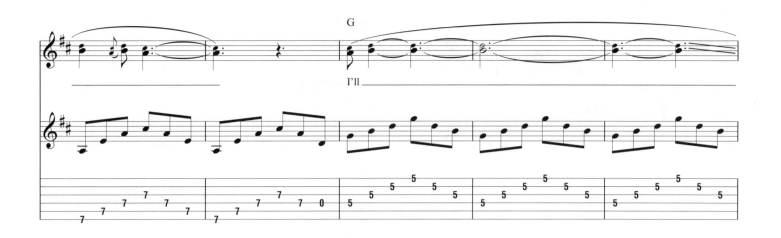

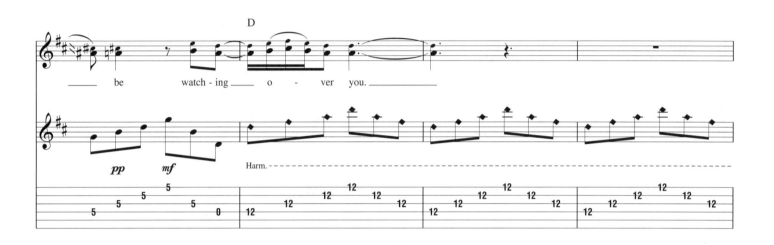

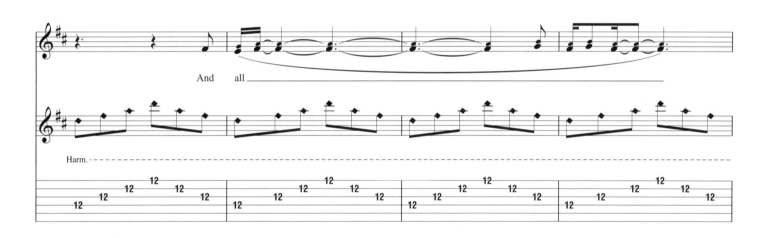

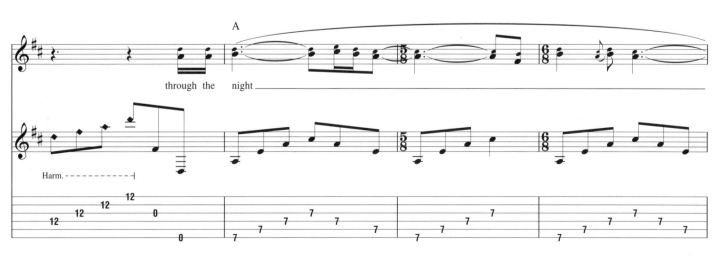

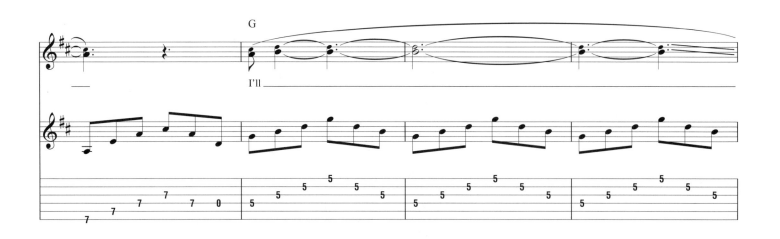

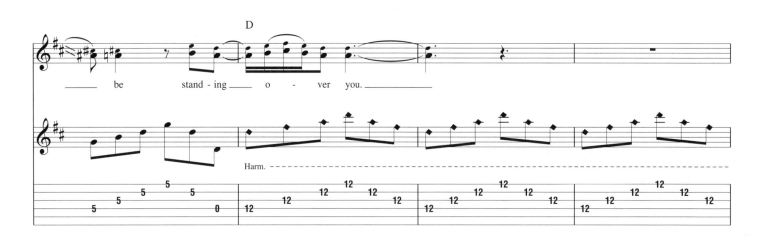

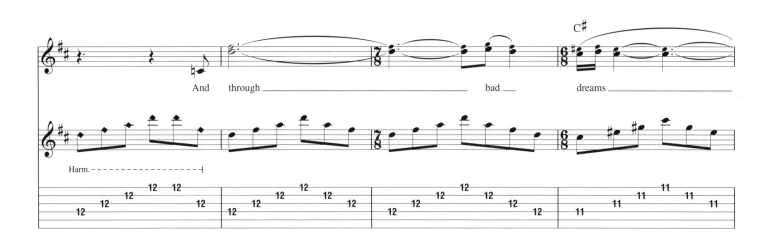

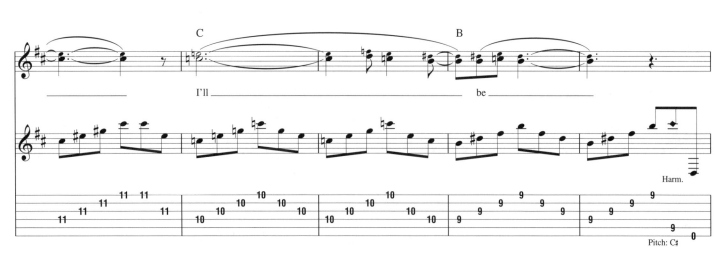

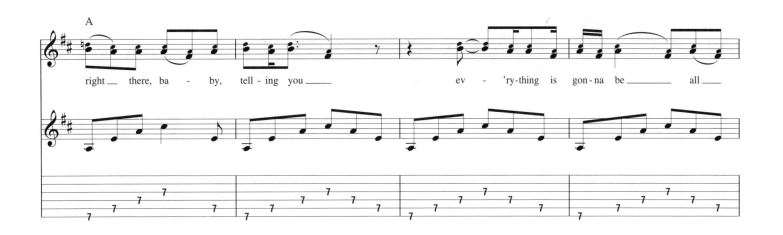

right __ there, ba - by, tell - ing you ____ ev - 'ry-thing is gon-na be ____ all __

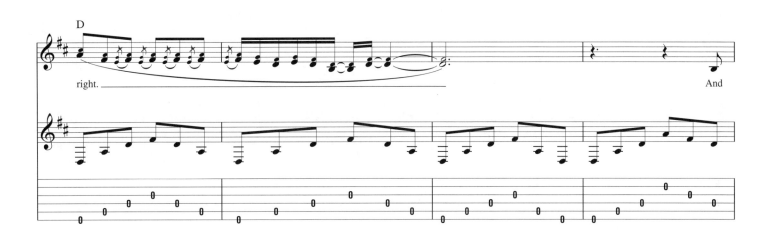

right. ____ And

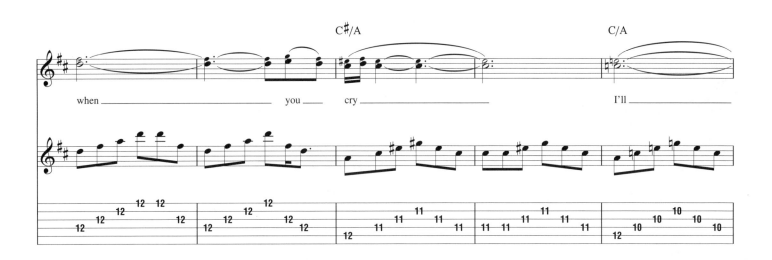

when ____ you __ cry ____ I'll __

be __ there, ba - by,

tell - ing you _____ you were nev - er noth - ing less _____ than _____ beau - ti - ful. _____

So don't _____

you wor - ry, _____ I'm your an - gel stand -

**A tempo**

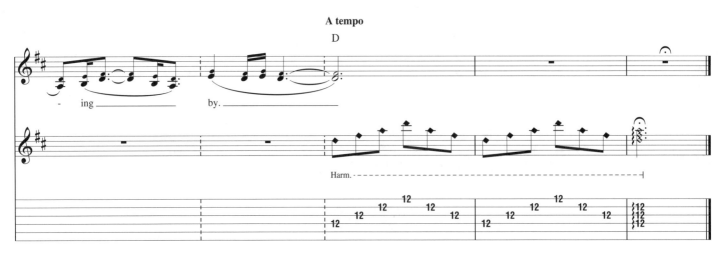

- ing _____ by.

# Break Me

### Words and Music by Jewel Kilcher

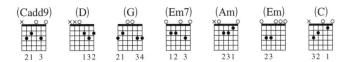

Capo I

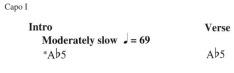

**Intro**
**Moderately slow** ♩ = 69
*Ab5

**Verse**
Ab5

*Chord symbols reflect overall harmony.

1. I will meet ___ you in some place ___

where the light lends it-self ___ to soft re-pose. ___ I will ___ let you

un - dress me, but I warn ___ you I have thorns like an-y rose. ___

**Verse**
Ab6
**(G6)
Ab5/G
(G5/F#)
Ab6/C
(G6/B)
Dbsus2
(Csus2)

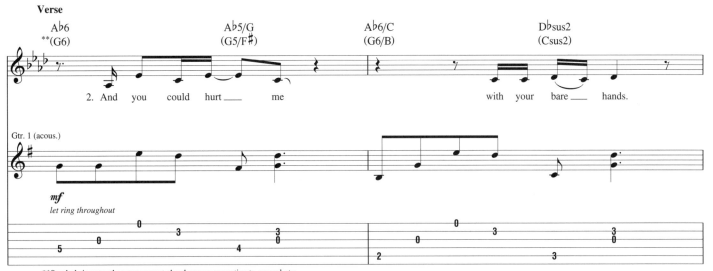

2. And you could hurt ___ me with your bare ___ hands.

Gtr. 1 (acous.)
*mf*
*let ring throughout*

**Symbols in parentheses represent chord names respective to capoed gtrs.
Symbols above represent actual sounding chords. Capoed fret is "0" in tab.
Chord symbols reflect implied harmony.

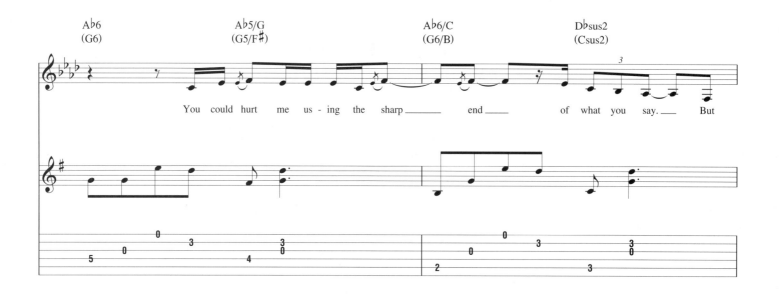

You could hurt me us - ing the sharp_____ end_____ of what you say._____ But

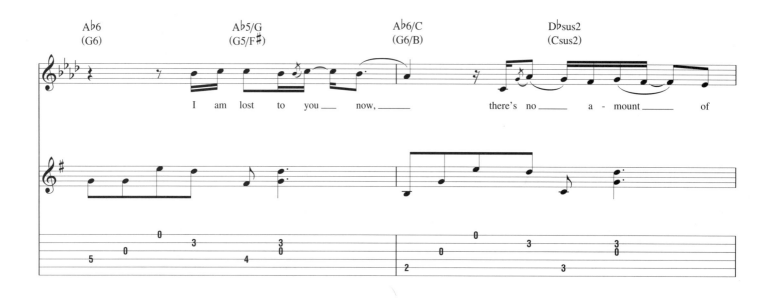

I am lost to you_____ now,_____ there's no_____ a - mount_____ of

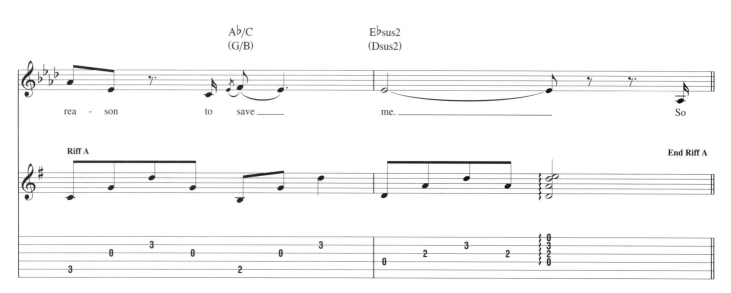

rea - son to save_____ me._____ So

**Riff A**

**End Riff A**

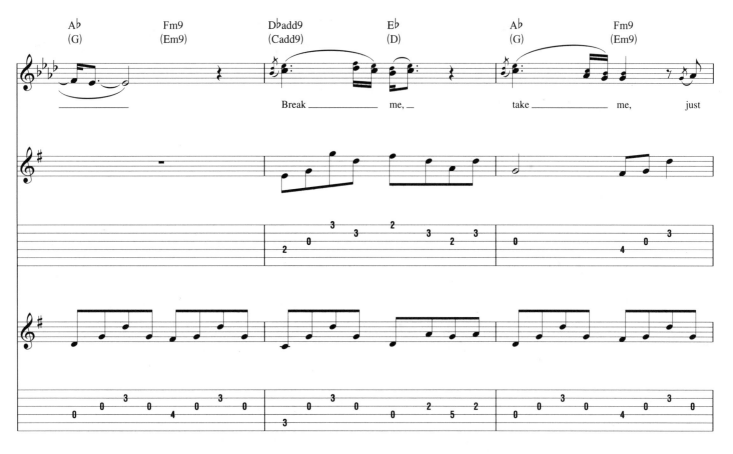

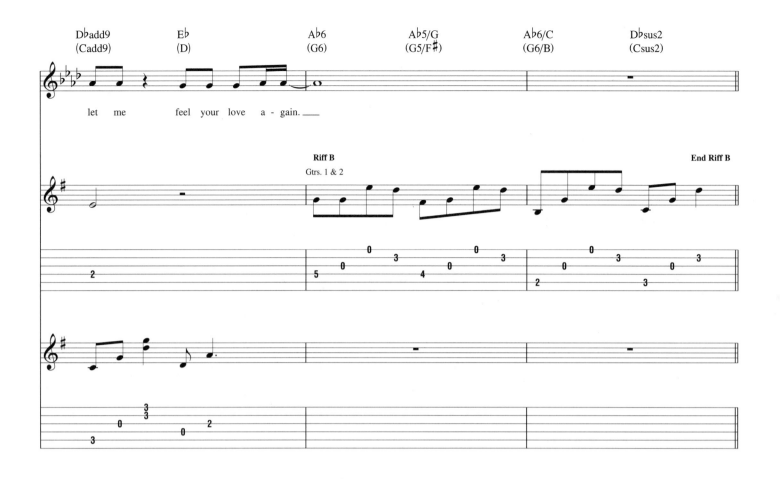

let me    feel your love a - gain. ___

**Riff B**
Gtrs. 1 & 2

**End Riff B**

**Verse**

Gtr. 1: w/ Riff B (3 times)
Gtr. 2 tacet

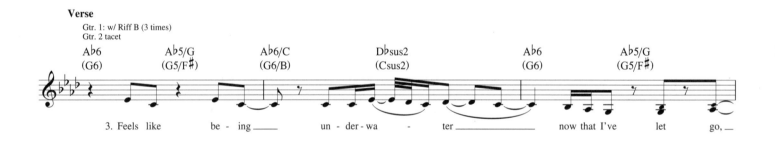

3. Feels like    be - ing ___ un - der - wa - ter ___ now that I've    let    go, ___

___ and lost con - trol. ___                Wa - ter kiss - es    fill ___ my mouth, ___ wa - ter,

Gtr. 2

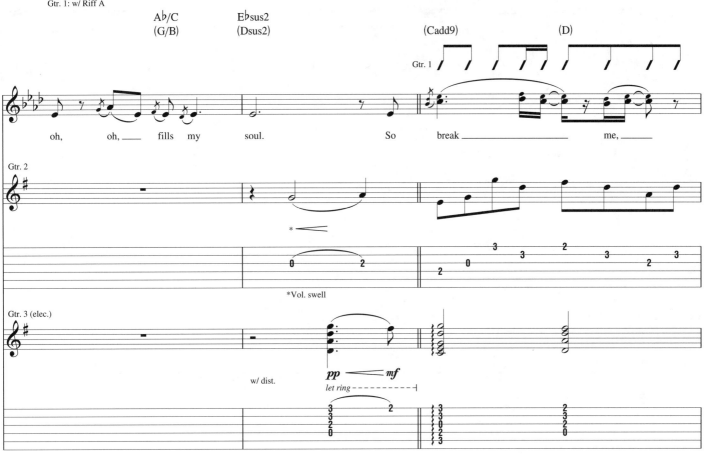

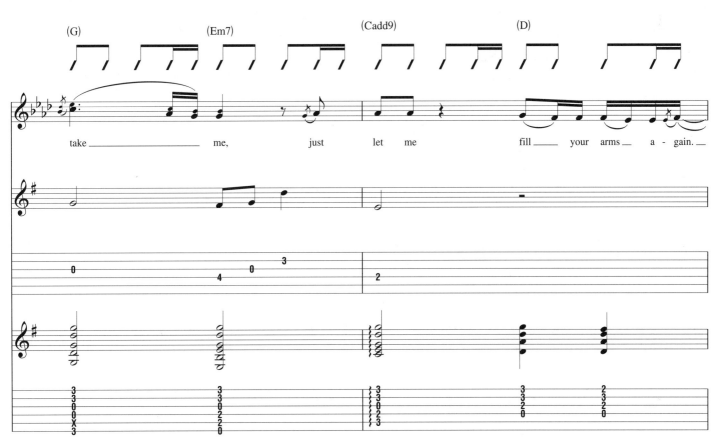

Break _____ me, I'll let you make me, just

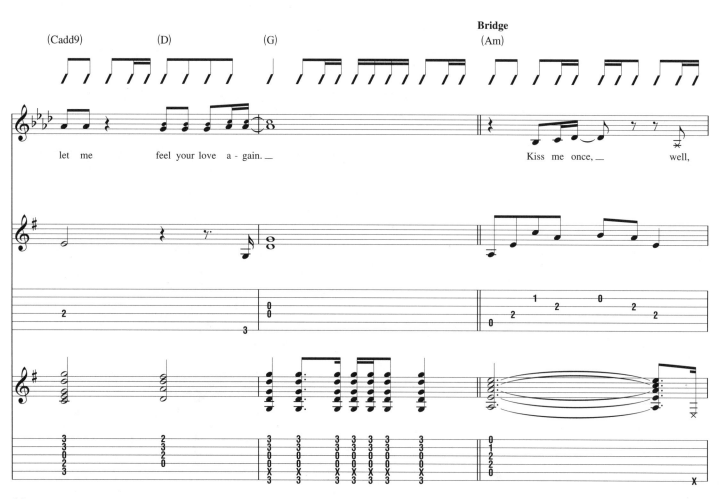

let me feel your love a - gain. ___

**Bridge**

Kiss me once, ___ well,

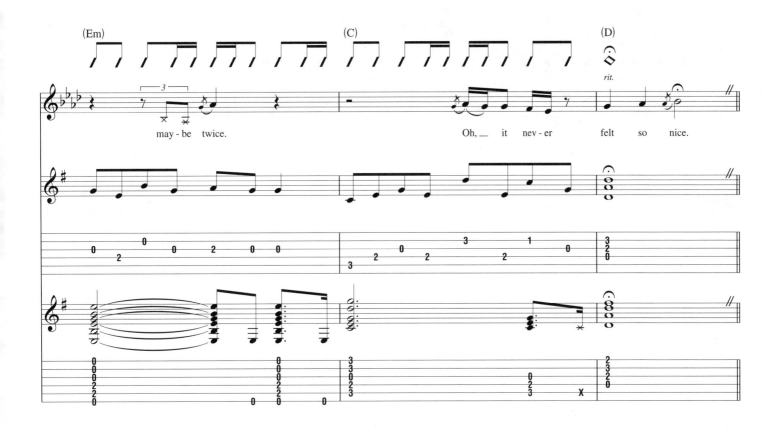

may - be twice.   Oh, ___ it nev - er felt so nice.

**Outro-Chorus**
**A tempo**

Gtrs, 1, 2 & 3 tacet

Break _____ me, _____ take _____ me, _____ just let me feel your love a - gain. ___

*Chord symbols reflect overall harmony (next 3 meas.).

Break _____ me, I'll let you, ooh, ___ I'll let you make ___ me, ___ just

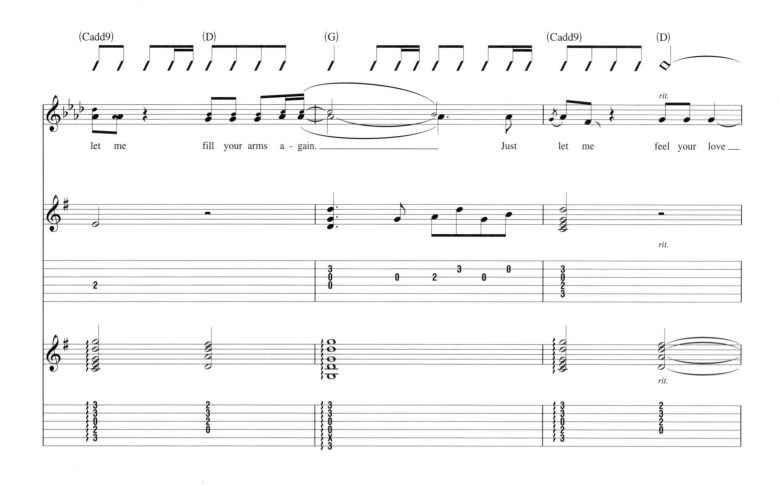

let me      fill your arms a - gain. _____     Just     let me     feel your love __

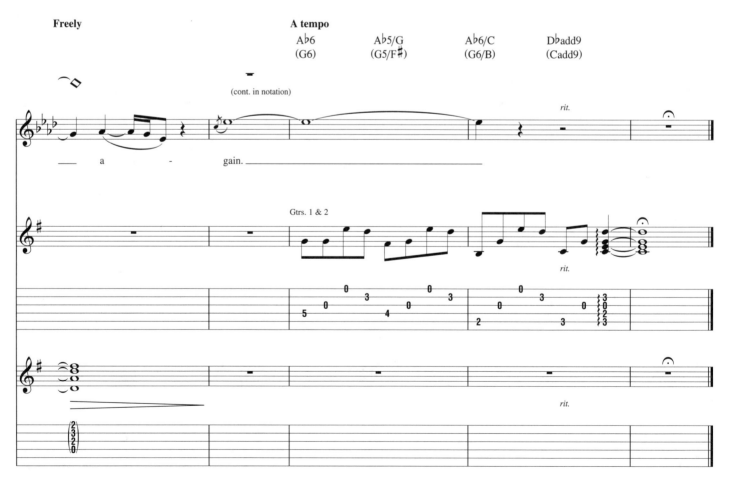

**Freely**                          **A tempo**

— a - gain. _____

# Foolish Games

**Words and Music by Jewel Kilcher**

**Intro**
**Moderately slow** ♩ = 88

*Piano arr. for gtr.
**Chord symbols reflect implied harmony.

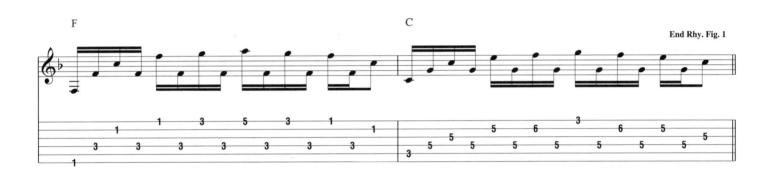

**Verse**

rain, _____ you're al - ways cra - zy like \_\_\_ that.
cig - a - rettes and talk - ing o - ver cof - fee.

**End Rhy. Fig. 2**

Gtr. 1: w/ Rhy. Fig. 2 (3 times)

And I watched \_ from my \_\_\_\_ win - dow, al - ways felt I was
Your phi - los - o - phies \_ on art, Ba - roque moved you. You loved Moz - art, \_ and you'd speak \_

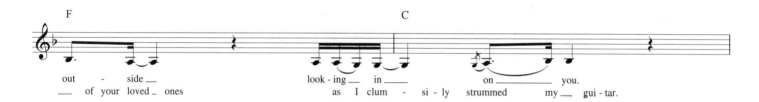

out - side \_ look - ing \_ in \_ on _____ you.
\_ of your loved \_ ones as I clum - si - ly strummed my \_ gui - tar.

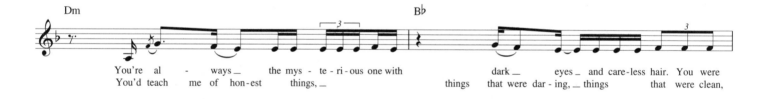

You're al - ways \_ the mys - te - ri - ous one with dark \_ eyes \_ and care - less hair. You were
You'd teach me of hon - est things, \_ things that were dar - ing, things that were clean,

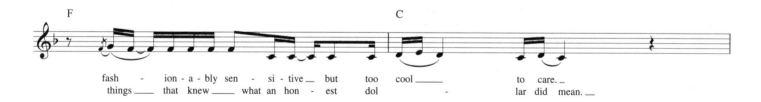

fash - ion - a - bly sen - si - tive \_ but too cool \_\_\_\_ to care. \_
things \_\_\_\_ that knew \_\_\_\_ what an hon - est dol - lar did mean. \_

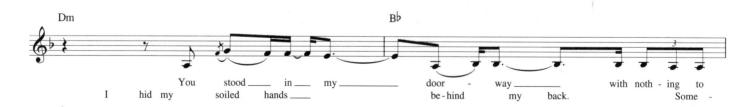

You stood \_\_\_\_ in my _____ door - way \_\_\_\_ with noth - ing to
I hid my soiled hands \_\_\_\_ be - hind my back. Some -

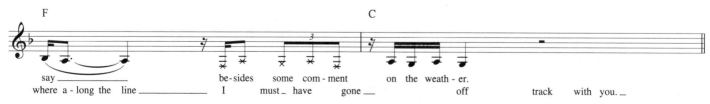

say _____ be - sides some com - ment on the weath - er.
where a - long the line _____ I must \_ have gone off track with you. \_

16

**Pre-Chorus**

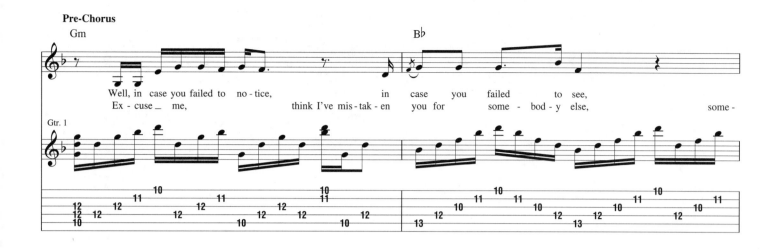

Well, in case you failed to no-tice, in case you failed to see,
Ex-cuse me, think I've mis-tak-en you for some-bod-y else, some-

this is my heart bleed-ing be-fore you, this is me down on my knees.
-bod-y who gave a damn, some-bod-y more like my-self.

**Chorus**

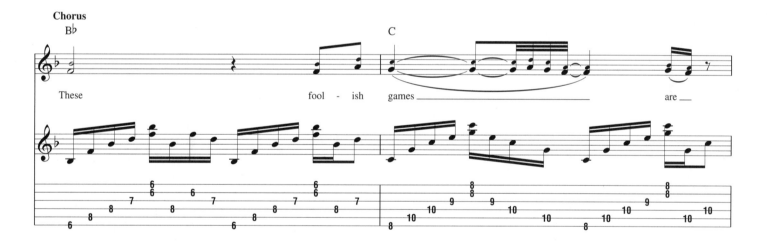

These fool-ish games are

tear-ing me a-part,
tear-ing me, you're tear-ing me, you're tear-ing me a-part, and

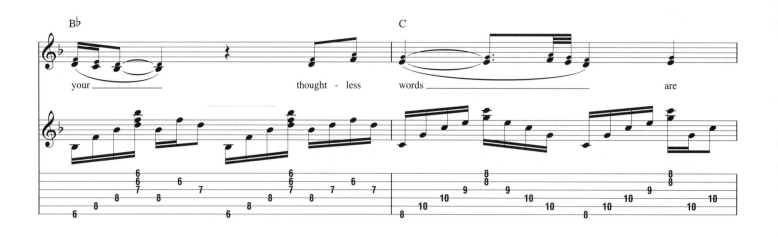

your _____ thought - less words _____ are

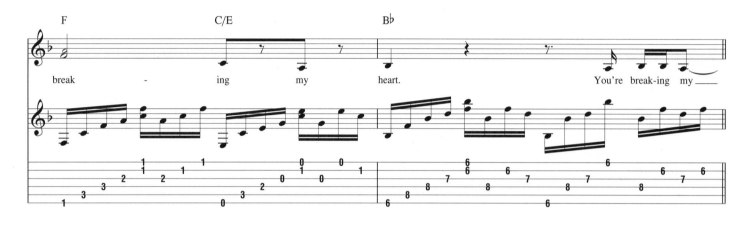

break - ing my heart. You're break-ing my _____

**Interlude**

Gtr. 1: w/ Rhy. Fig. 1

_____ heart.

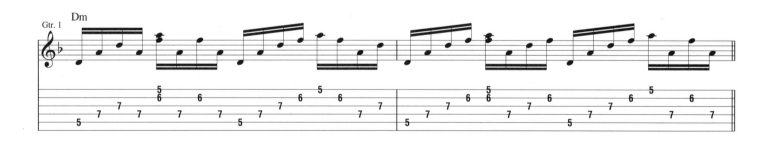

**Verse**

Gtr. 1: w/ Rhy. Fig. 2

3. You took your coat off, ___ stood in the rain, ___ you're al-ways cra - zy ___ like that.

*Repeat & fade*

**Outro**

Gtr. 1: w/ Rhy. Fig. 1

from *Spirit*

# Hands

**Words and Music by Patrick Leonard and Jewel Kilcher**

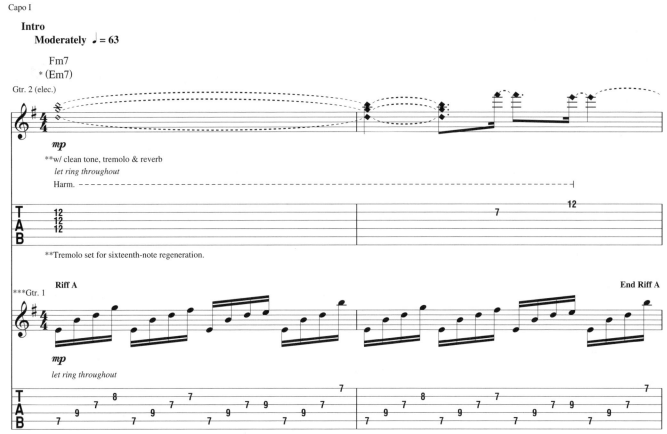

*Symbols in parentheses represent chord names respective to capoed gtrs.
Symbols above represent actual sounding chords. Capoed fret is "0" in tab.
Chord symbols reflect implied harmony.

***Piano arr. for gtr.

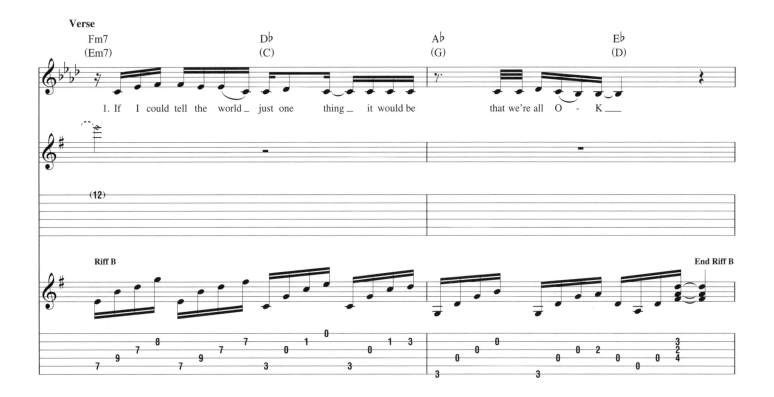

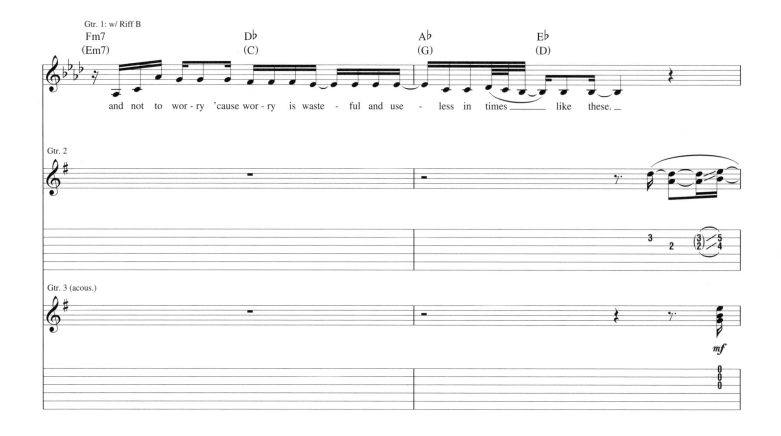

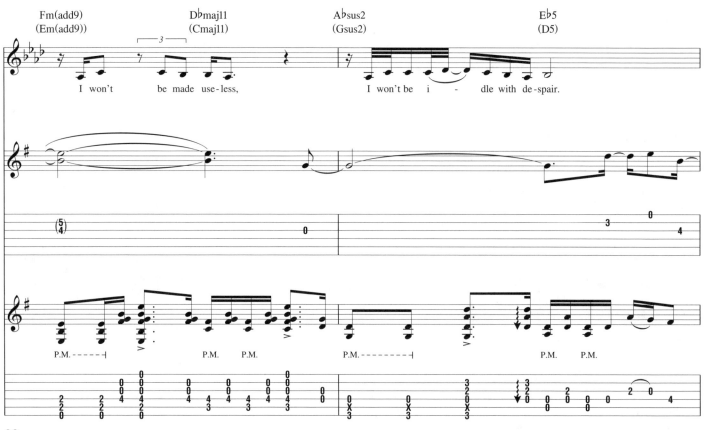

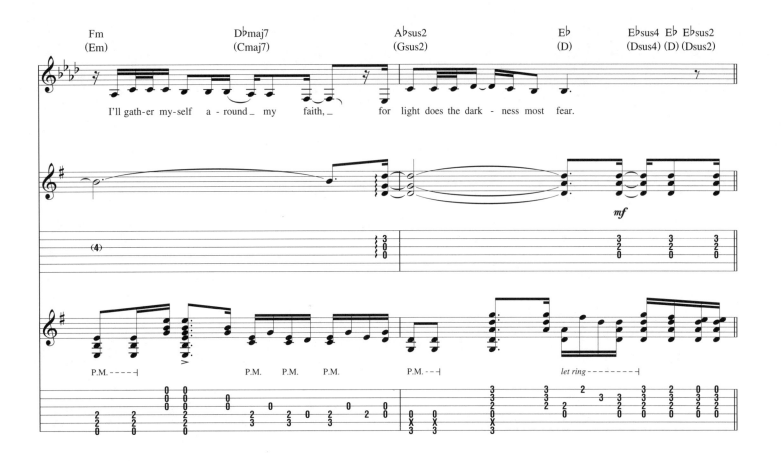

I'll gath-er my-self a-round my faith, for light does the dark-ness most fear.

**Chorus**

My hands are small, I know, but they're not yours, they are my own. But they're

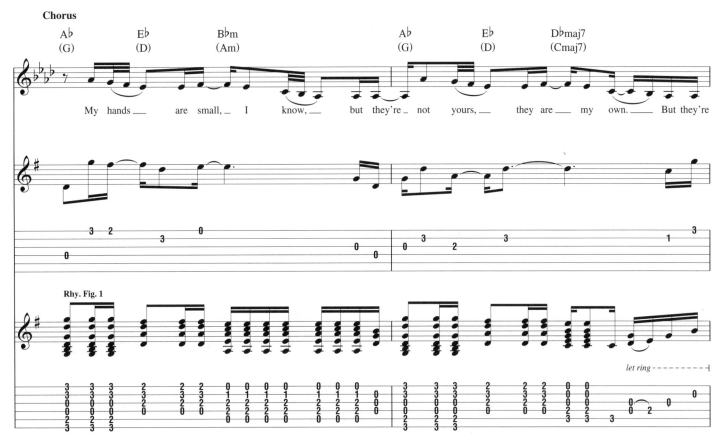

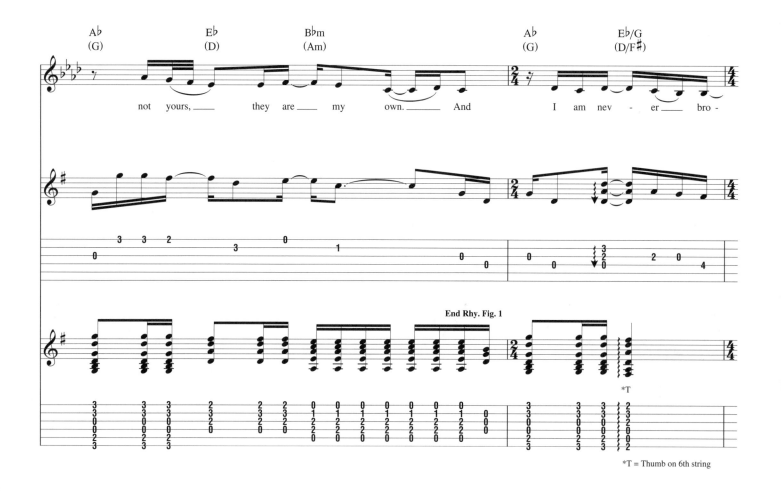

not yours, \_\_\_\_ they are \_\_\_ my own. \_\_\_ And

I am nev - er \_\_\_ bro -

End Rhy. Fig. 1

*T = Thumb on 6th string

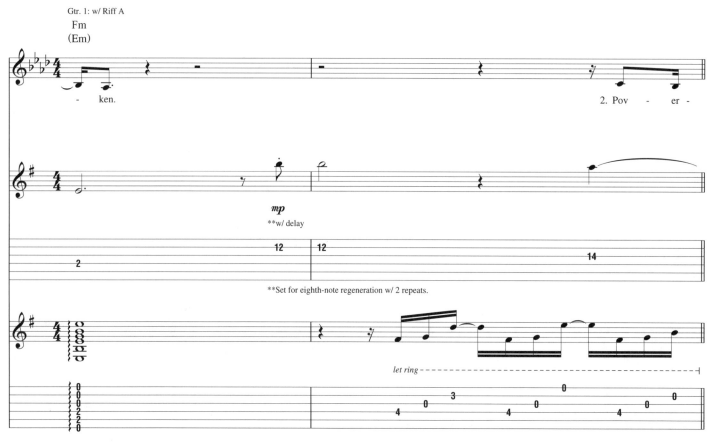

Gtr. 1: w/ Riff A

- ken.

2. Pov - er -

*mp*

**w/ delay

**Set for eighth-note regeneration w/ 2 repeats.

let ring - - - - - - - - - - - - - - - - - - - - - - - - -

22

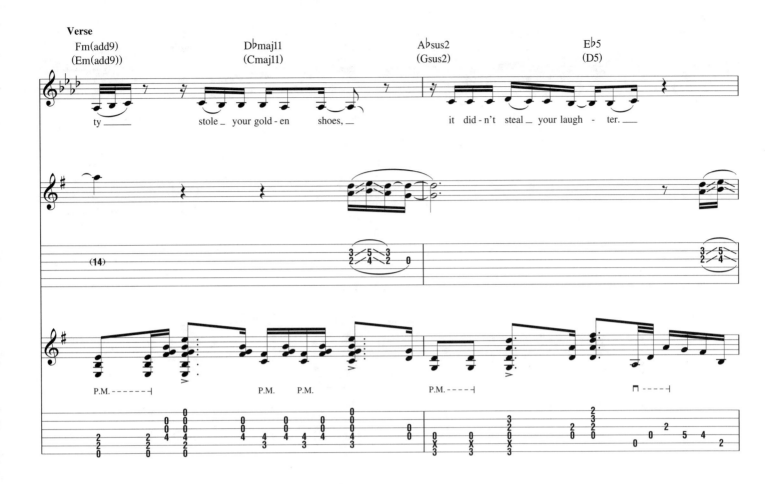

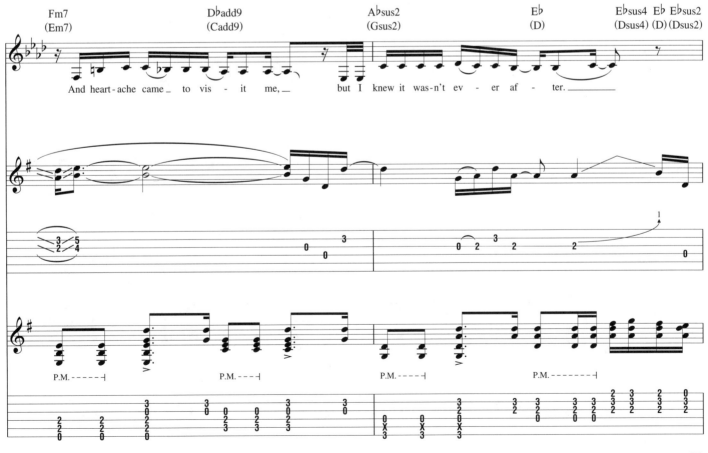

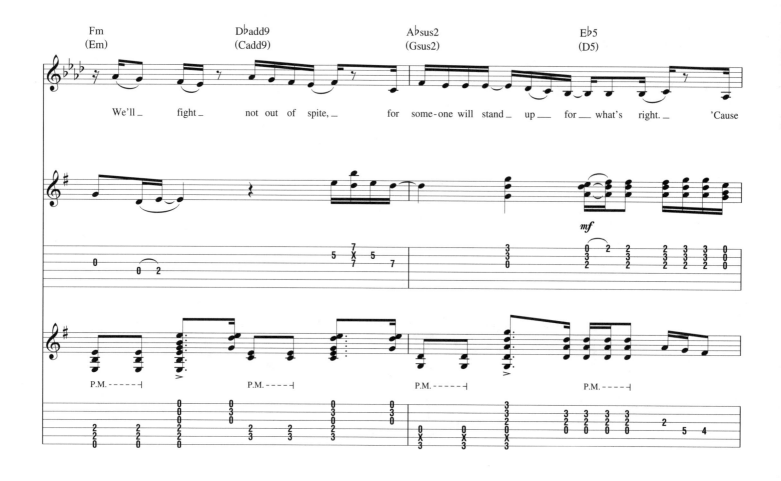

We'll _ fight _ not out of spite, _ for some-one will stand _ up _ for _ what's right. _ 'Cause

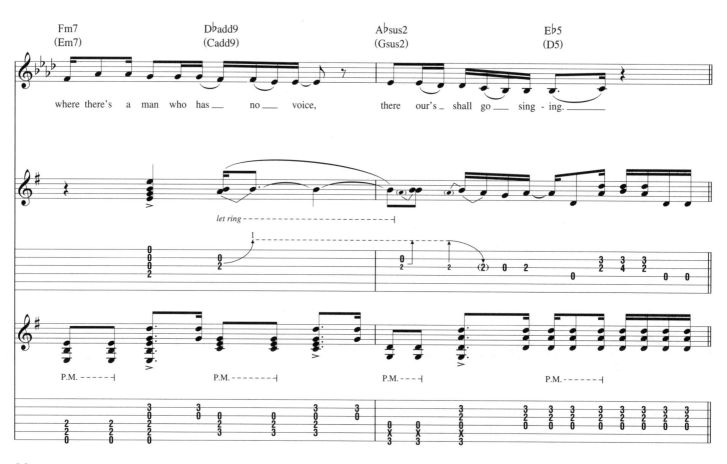

where there's a man who has _ no _ voice, there our's _ shall go _ sing - ing. _

**Chorus**

Gtr. 3: w/ Rhy. Fig. 1

My hands __ are small, _ I know, __ but they're _ not yours, __ they are __ my own. ____ But they're

Voc. Fig. 1

(Ah. _____ ) Ah. _____

Gtr. 2

not yours, __ they are __ my own. ____ And I am nev - er bro - ken. __

End Voc. Fig. 1

Ah.) _____

Gtr. 2

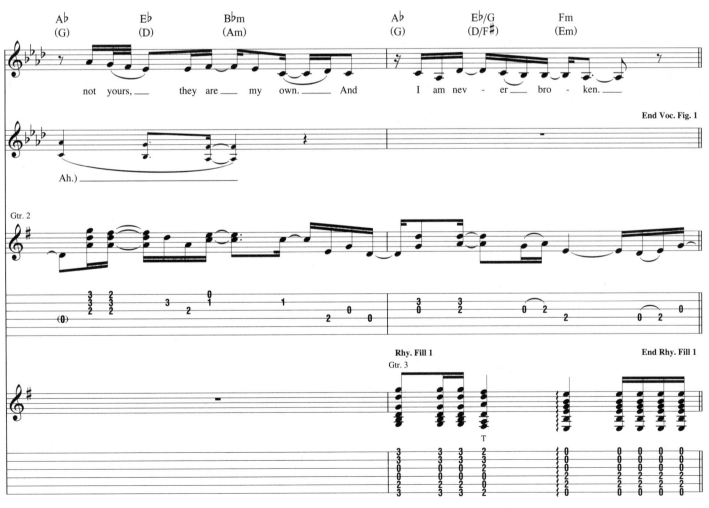

Rhy. Fill 1          End Rhy. Fill 1

Gtr. 3

**Bridge**

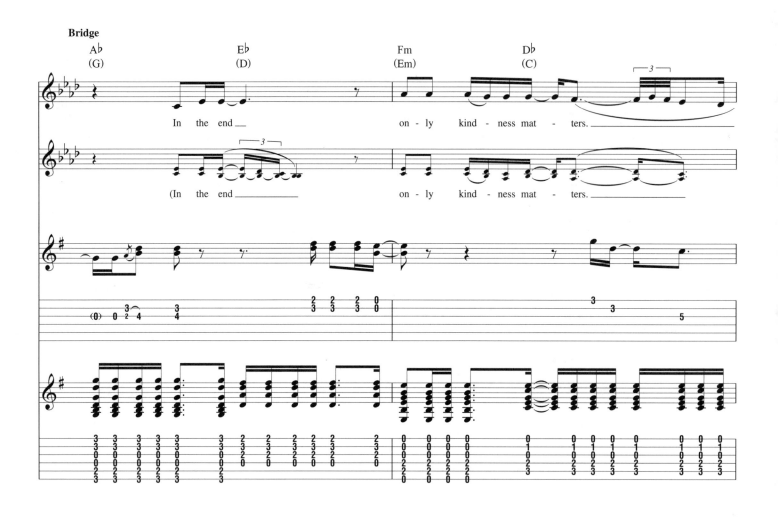

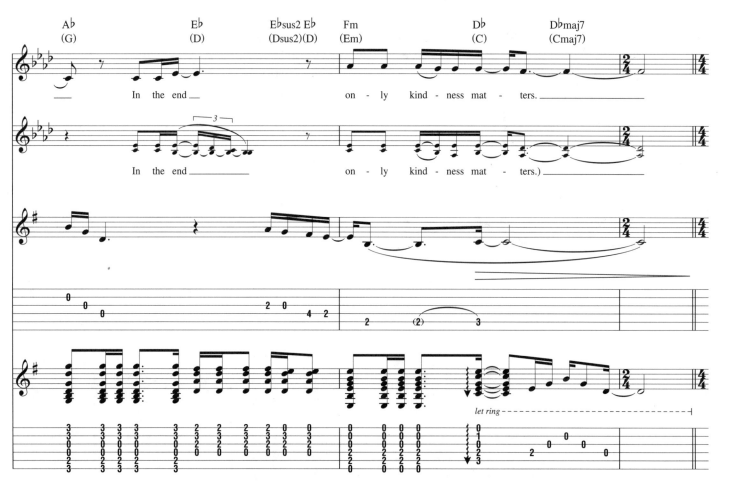

**Verse**

Gtr. 1: w/ Riff B (3 times)
Gtr. 3 tacet

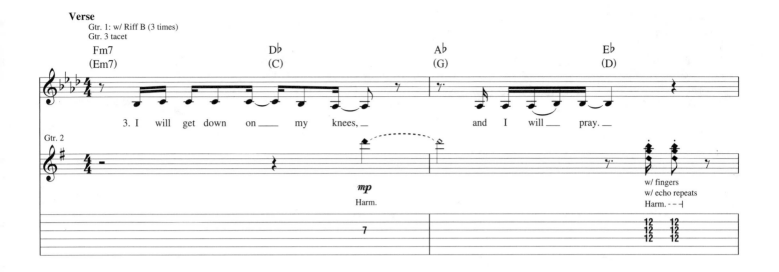

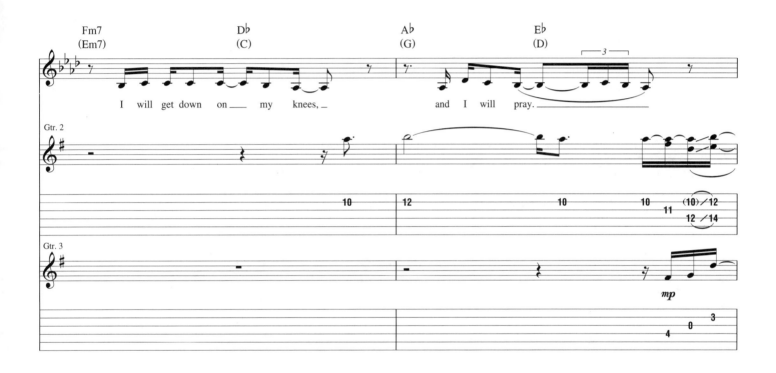

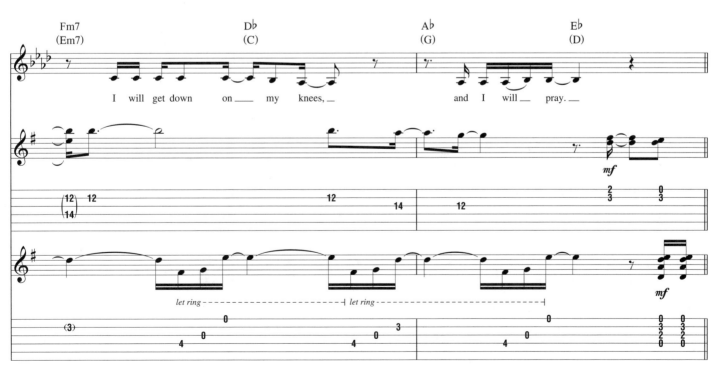

27

**Chorus**

Bkgd. Voc.: w/ Voc. Fig. 1 (2 times)
Gtr. 3: w/ Rhy. Fig. 1

My hands ___ are small, ___ I know, ___ but they're ___ not yours, ___ they are ___ my own. ___ But they're ___

Gtr. 2

Gtr. 3: w/ Rhy. Fill 1

___ not yours, ___ they are my ___ own. ___ And I am nev - er bro - ken. ___

Gtr. 3: w/ Rhy. Fig. 1

My hands ___ are small, ___ I know, ___ but they're ___ not yours, ___ they are ___ my own. ___ But they're

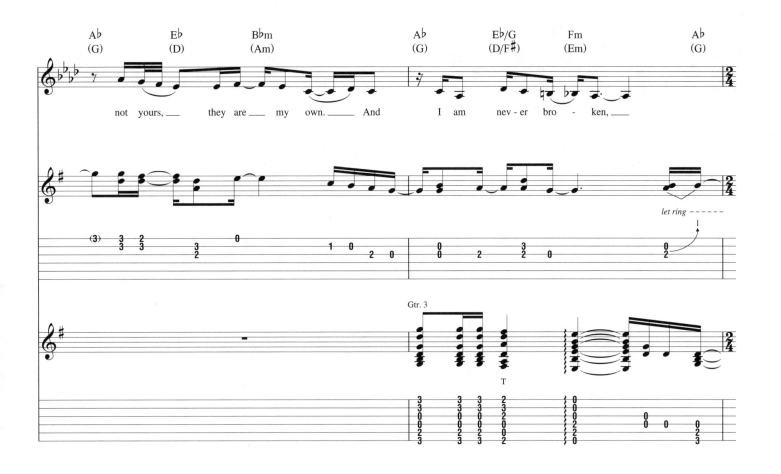

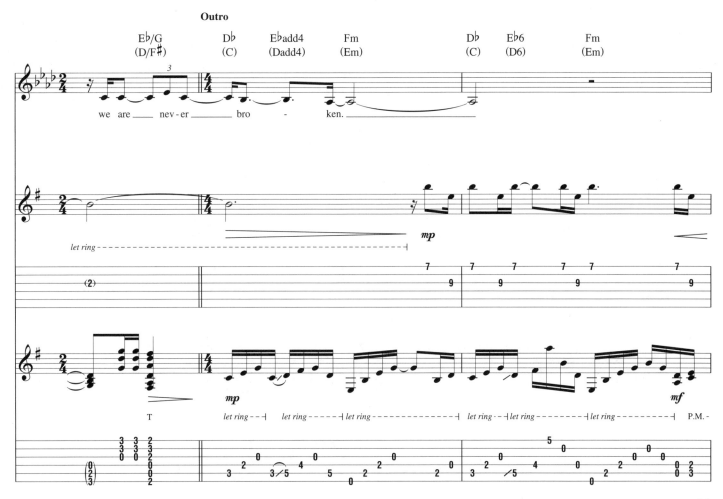

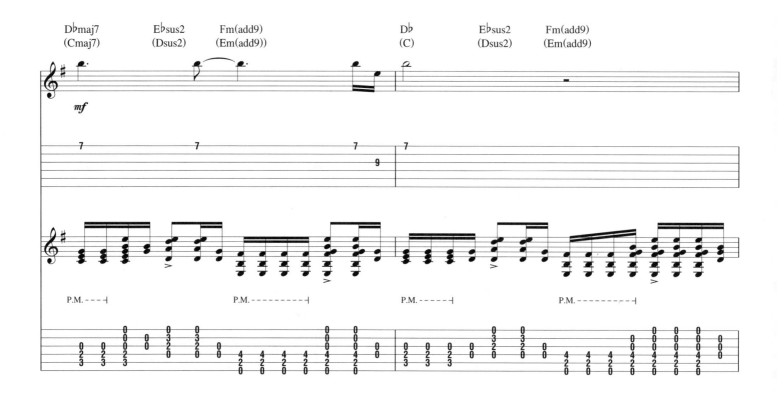

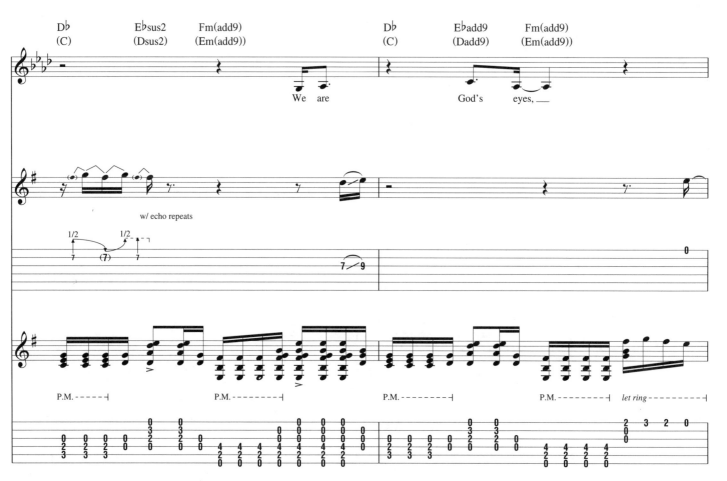

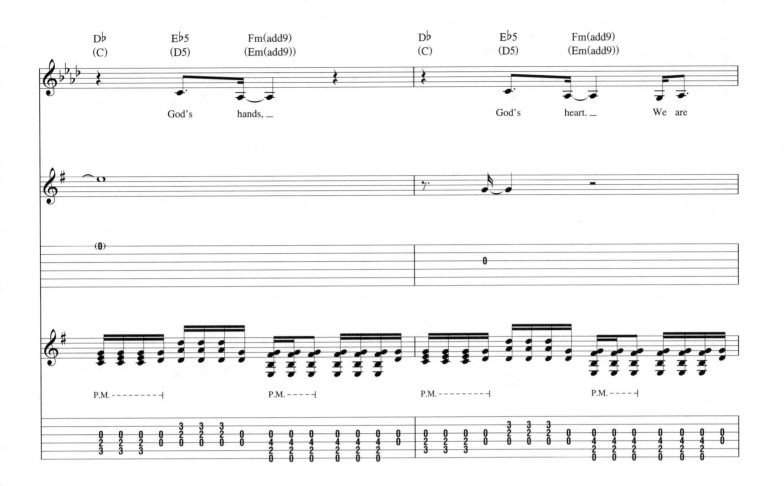

***Begin fade***

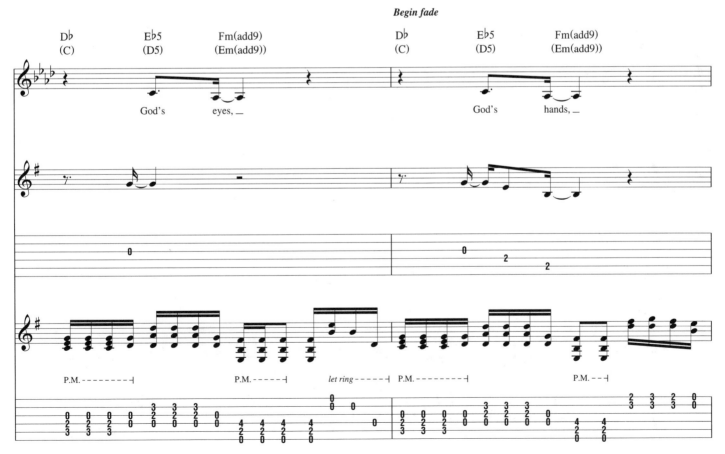

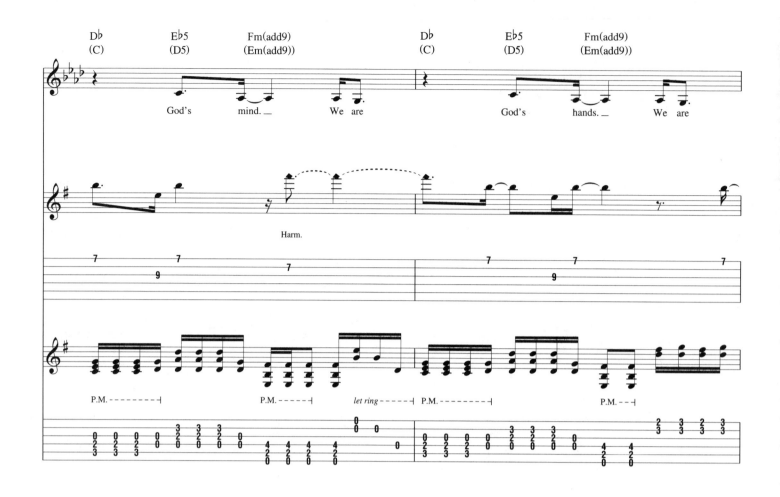

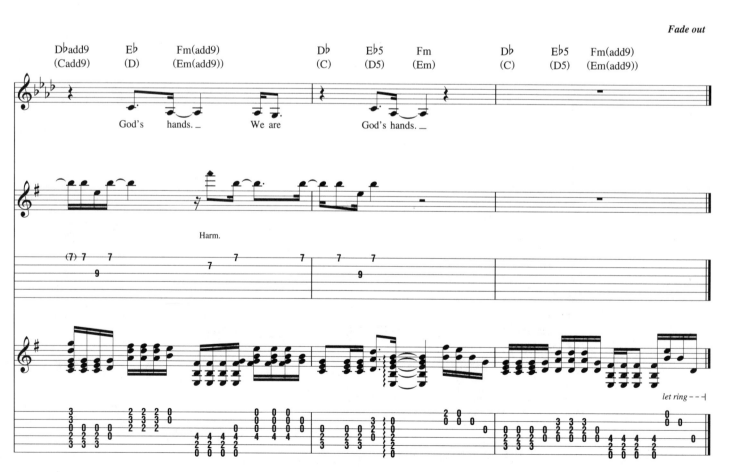

from *0304*

# Intuition

### Words and Music by Jewel Kilcher and Lester A. Mendez

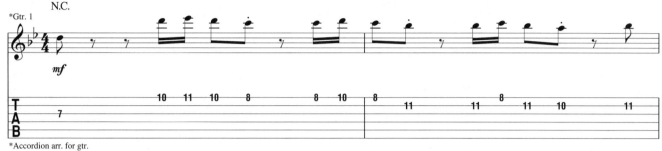

Gtrs. 2 & 3: Capo III

**Intro**
**Moderate Rock** ♩ = 96

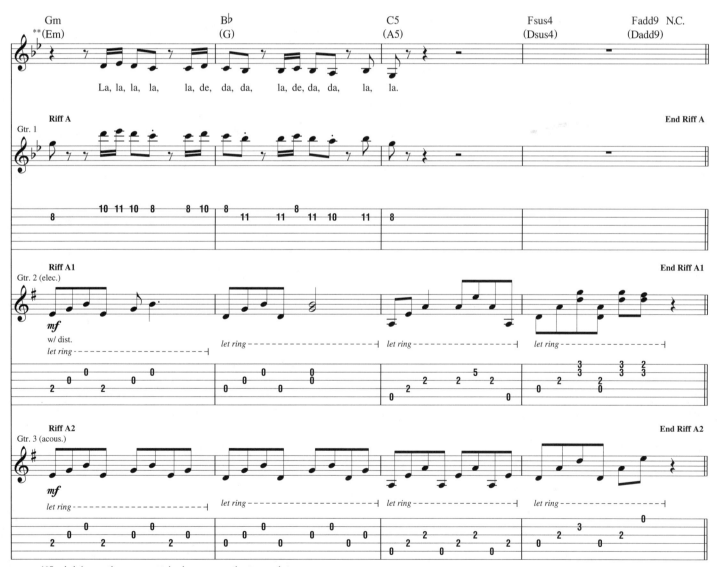

**\*Accordion arr. for gtr.**

\*\*Symbols in parentheses represent chord names respective to capoed gtrs.
Symbols above reflect actual sounding chords. Capoed fret is "0" in tab.
Chord symbols reflect implied harmony.

**Verse**

Gtrs. 1 & 2 tacet

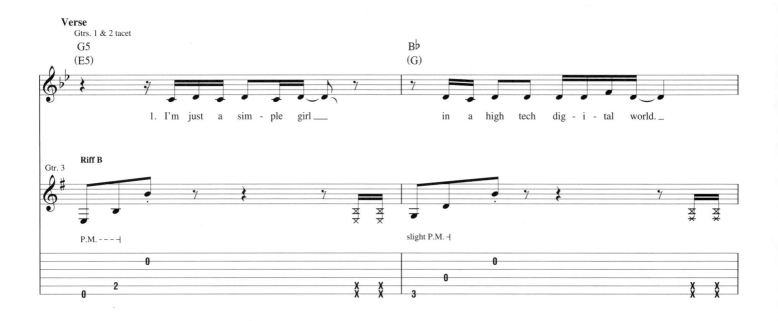

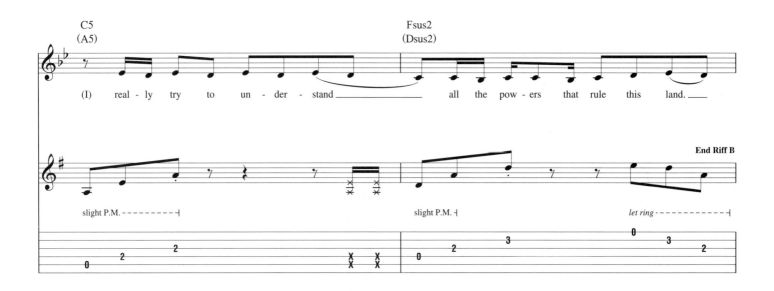

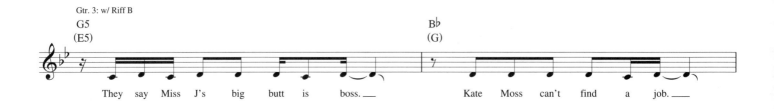

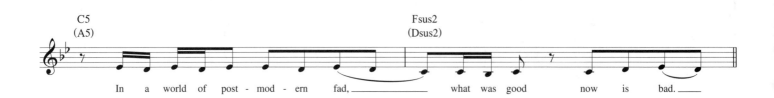

**Pre-Chorus**

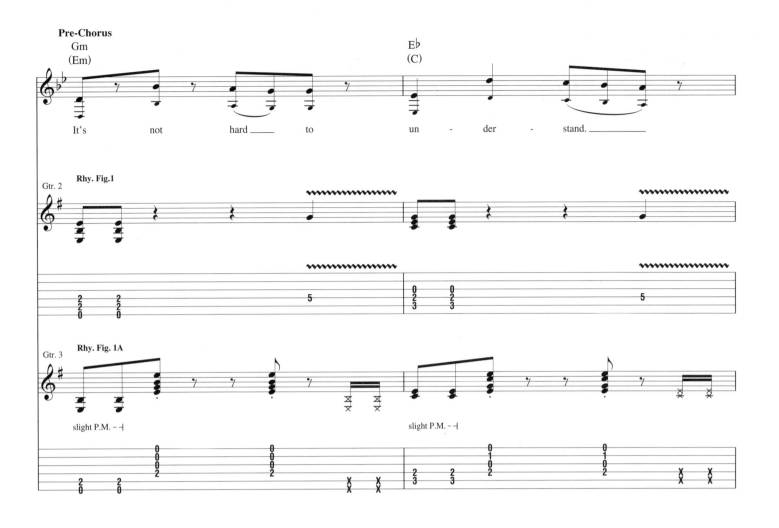

It's   not   hard ____ to   un - der - stand. ____

just   fol - low ____ this ____   sim - ple   plan. ____

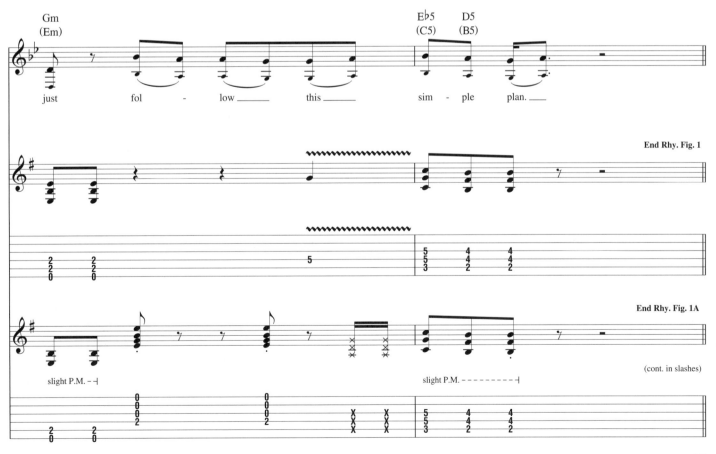

**Chorus**

Fol-low your heart, _____ your in - tu - i - tion, it will lead you in _____

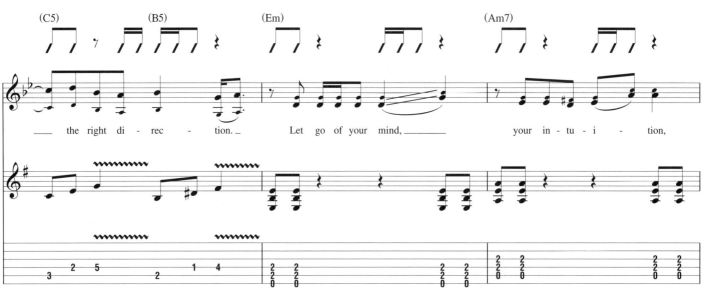

_____ the right di - rec - tion. _____ Let go of your mind, _____ your in - tu - i - tion,

it's eas - y to find, _____ just fol - low your heart, ba - by. _____

**Interlude**
Gtrs. 1, 2 & 3: w/ Riffs A, A1 & A2

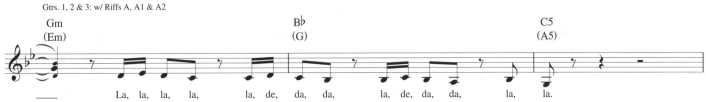

La, la, la, la,   la, de, da, da,   la, de, da, da,   la,   la.

**Verse**
Gtr. 3: w/ Riff B

2. You looked at me but you're not quite sure.

Am I it or could you get more?   You learned cool from mag - a - zines. _____

You learned love from Char - lie Sheen. ___   If   you ___ want ___ me,

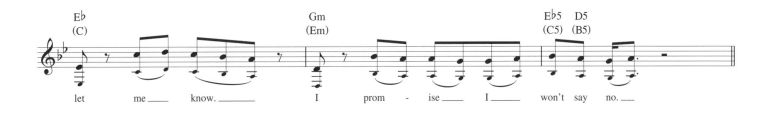

let   me ___ know. ___   I   prom - ise ___ I   won't say no. ___

**Chorus**
Gtrs. 2 & 3: w/ Rhy. Figs. 2 & 2A

Fol - low your heart, ___   your in - tu - i - tion,   it will lead you in ___

___ the right di - rec - tion. ___   Let go of your mind, ___   your in - tu - i - tion,

37

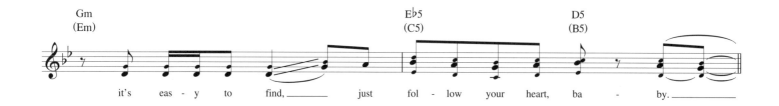

it's eas-y to find, _____ just fol-low your heart, ba - by. _____

**Bridge**

You got some-thing that you're want-ing to sell.

Gtr. 1  **Riff C**

Gtr. 3  **Rhy. Fig. 3**

*mf*

*let ring - - - - -|*

Sell your sin, just cash in.

**End Riff C**

*let ring - - - - - - |*

**End Rhy. Fig. 3**

Gtr. 1: w/ Riff C
Gtr. 3: w/ Rhy. Fig. 3

You got some-thing that you're want-ing to tell.

Gtr. 3: w/ Rhy. Fig 1A

You'll love me, wait and see.___ If you want me ___ don't ___ play ___ games.___

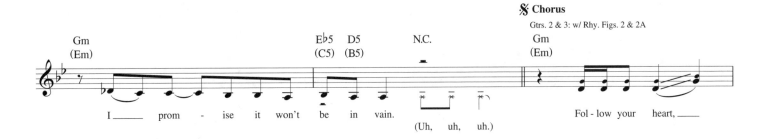

**𝄋 Chorus**

Gtrs. 2 & 3: w/ Rhy. Figs. 2 & 2A

I ___ prom - ise it won't be in vain. (Uh, uh, uh.) Fol - low your heart,___

your in - tu - i - tion, it will lead you in ___ the right di - rec - tion.___

Let go of your mind,___ your in - tu - i - tion, it's eas - y to find,___ just

**To Coda ⊕**
**Interlude**

fol - low your heart, ba - by.___ Just fol-low your ___ heart,___ your in - tu - i - tion,

Gtr. 2

*mp*

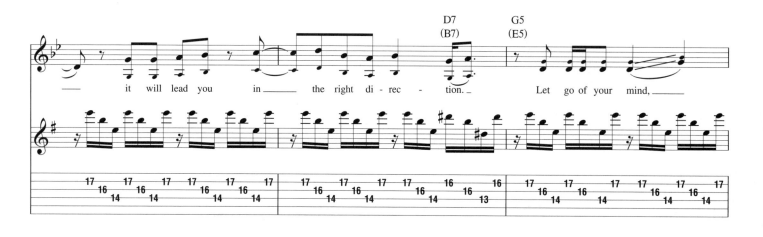

*D.S. al Coda*

**⊕ Coda**

**Outro-Chorus**

Gtr. 2: w/ Rhy. Fig. 2 (1 1/2 times)
Gtr. 3: w/ Rhy. Fig. 2A (1 3/8 times)

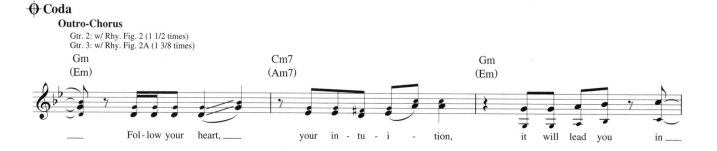

# Jesus Loves You (What About Me)

### Words and Music by Jewel Kilcher

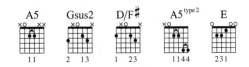

**Chorus**

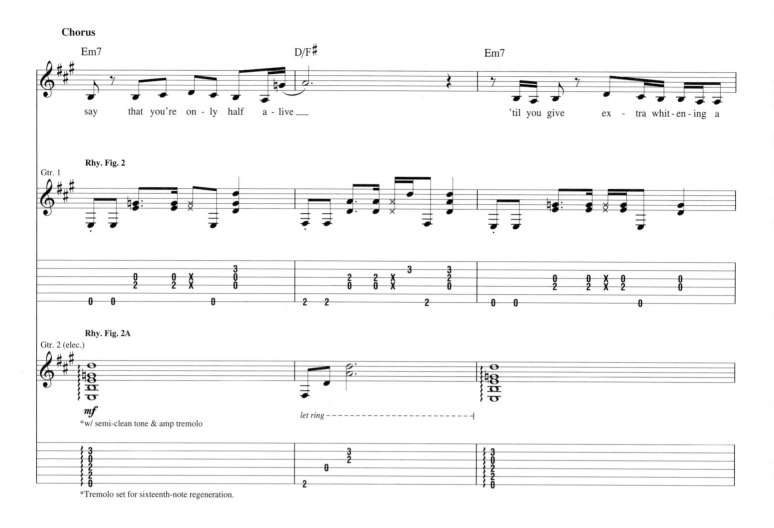

say that you're on-ly half a-live ___ 'til you give ex - tra whit-en-ing a

**Rhy. Fig. 2**
Gtr. 1

**Rhy. Fig. 2A**
Gtr. 2 (elec.)

*mf*
*w/ semi-clean tone & amp tremolo

*let ring - - - - - - - - - - - - - - - - - - - - - - - - |

*Tremolo set for sixteenth-note regeneration.

try. ___ Well, I wan-na see, ___ I wan-na see, ___

*let ring - - - - - - - - - - - - - - - - - - - - - |

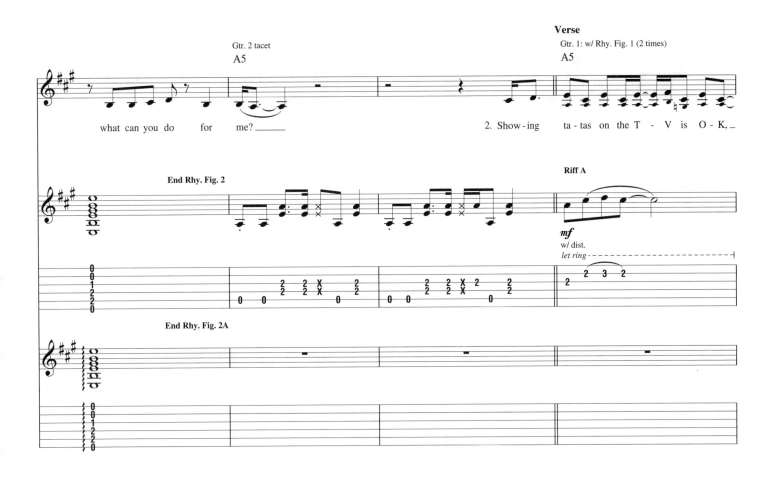

what can you do    for    me? ___

**Verse**

Gtr. 2 tacet
A5

Gtr. 1: w/ Rhy. Fig. 1 (2 times)
A5

2. Show-ing    ta-tas    on the T - V is O - K, __

End Rhy. Fig. 2

Riff A

mf
w/ dist.
let ring - - - - - - - - - - - - - - - - - - - -

End Rhy. Fig. 2A

Gtr. 3: w/ Riff A (3 times)
Gsus2

I wan-na    be O - K    too. ___

And hav-ing my

End Riff A    Riff B
Gtr. 4 (elec.)

End Riff B

Gtr. 3

let ring - - - - - - - - - - - - - - - -

pp ————————— mf
w/ dist.
fdbk.
*

Pitch: C#

*Using a guitar with Les Paul-style electronics, set lead volume to 0 and rhythm
volume to 10. Strike the string while the pickup selector is in the lead position,
then flip the switch in the rhythm indicated to simulate the re-attack.

Gtr. 4 tacet
A5

Gtr. 4: w/ Riff B
Gsus2

pic-ture  in  a  mag - a-zine makes me ___  spe - cial.  How spe-cial are    you?

They

**Chorus**

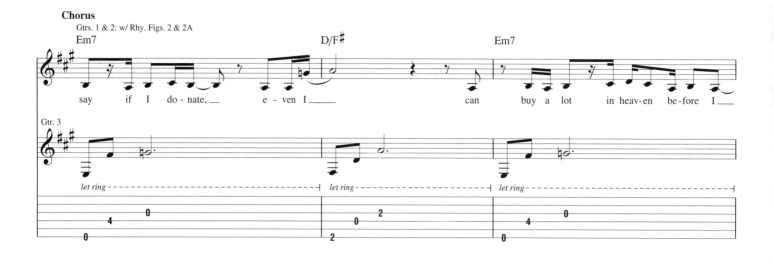

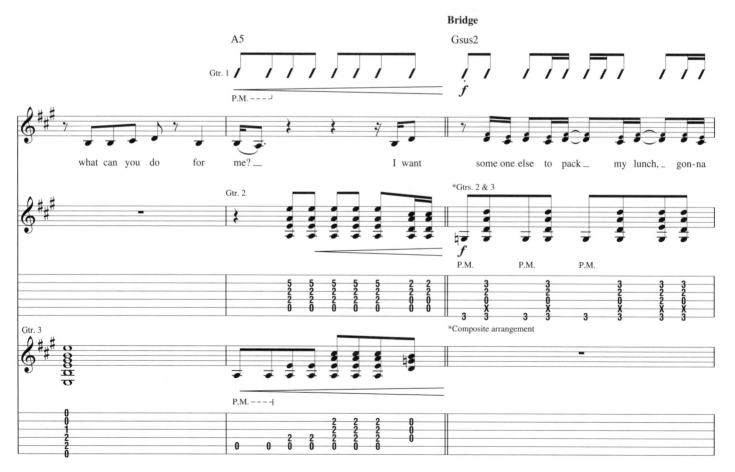

get some-one else to pull the punch. Oh,

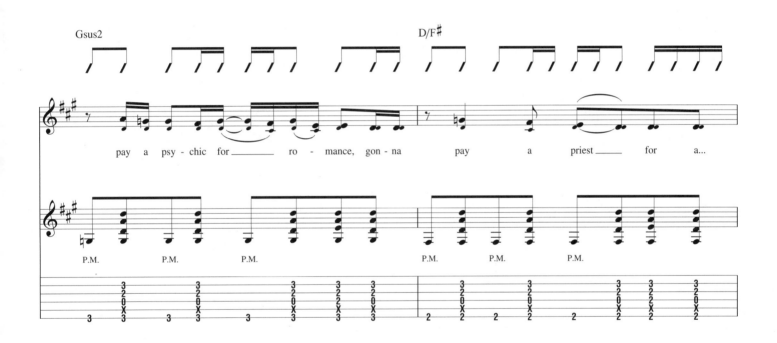

pay a psy-chic for ro - mance, gon-na pay a priest for a...

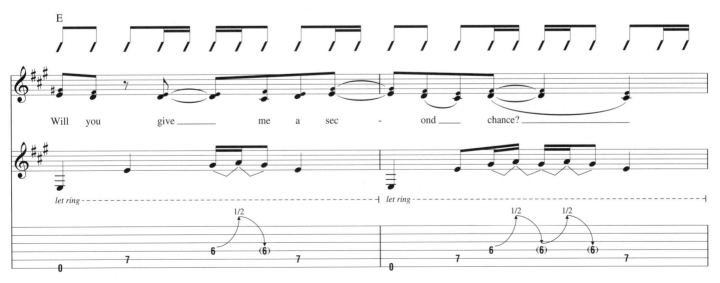

Will you give me a sec - ond chance?

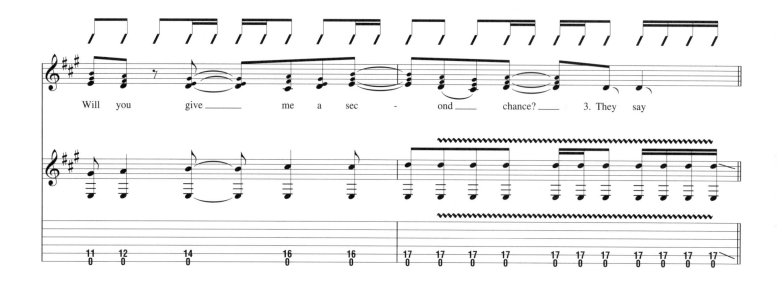

Will you give me a sec - ond chance? 3. They say

**Verse**

Gtr. 1: w/ Rhy. Fig. 1 (2 times)
Gtrs. 2 & 3 tacet

A5

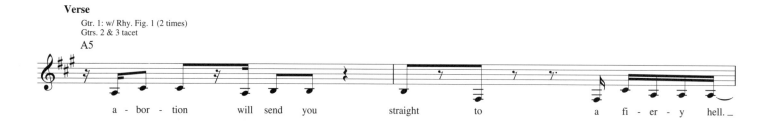

a - bor - tion will send you straight to a fi - er - y hell.

Gsus2

Gtr. 4: w/ Riff B (2 times)

A5

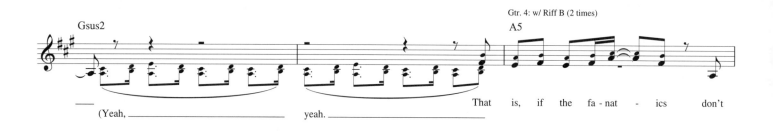

(Yeah, yeah. That is, if the fa - nat - ics don't

Gsus2

beat Sa - tan to the kill. Yeah, yeah.)

**Chorus**

Gtr. 1: w/ Rhy. Fig. 2 (1st 3 meas.)
Gtr. 2: w/ Rhy. Fig. 2A

Em7          D/F#          Em7

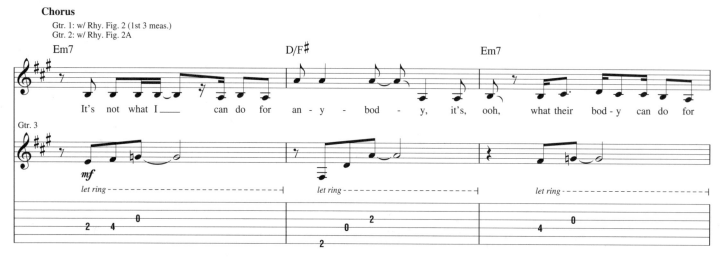

It's not what I can do for an - y - bod - y, it's, ooh, what their bod - y can do for

Gtr. 3

*mf*

*let ring* - - - - - - - - - - - - - - - - *let ring* - - - - - - - - - - - - - - - - *let ring* - - - - - - - - - - - - - - - -

46

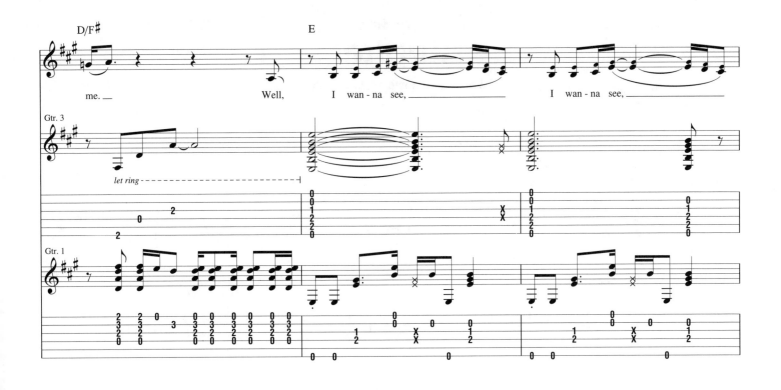

from *Spirit*

# Jupiter

### Words and Music by Jewel Kilcher

Gtr. 1: Open Dsus2 tuning:
(low to high) D-A-D-E-A-E

Gtrs. 2 & 3: Capo II

**Intro**

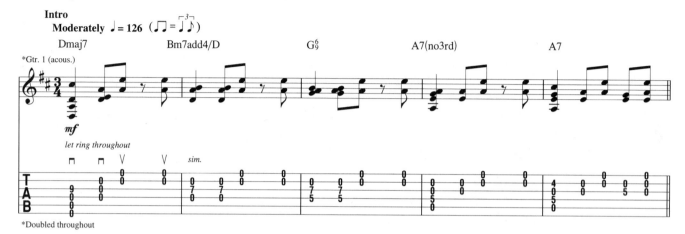

**Verse**

1. Ve - nus de Mi - lo in her half - baked shell un - der - stood _ the

na - ture of ___ love ver - y well. ___ She said, "A good love is ___ de -

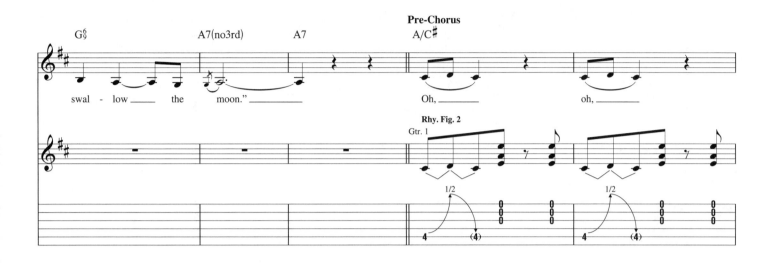

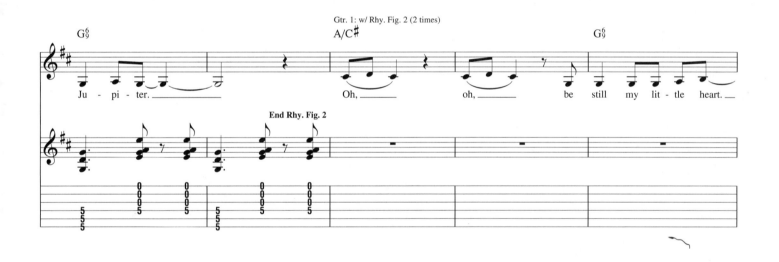

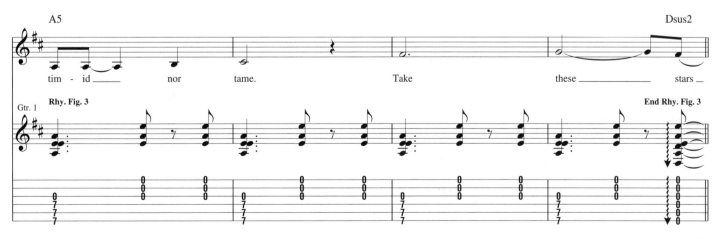

**Chorus**

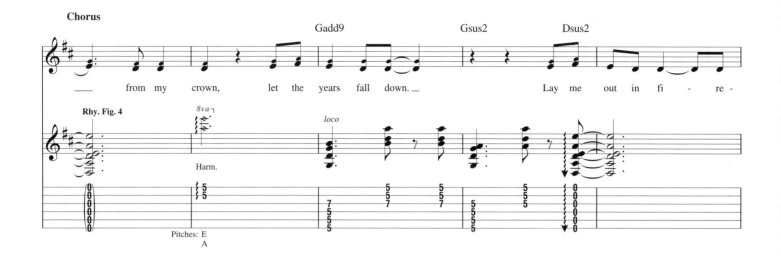

from my crown, let the years fall down. ___ Lay me out in fi - re -

light, let my skin feel _____ the night. Fas - ten me to your side, _____

say it will be _____ soon. _____ You make me so _____ cra - zy, ba - by, could

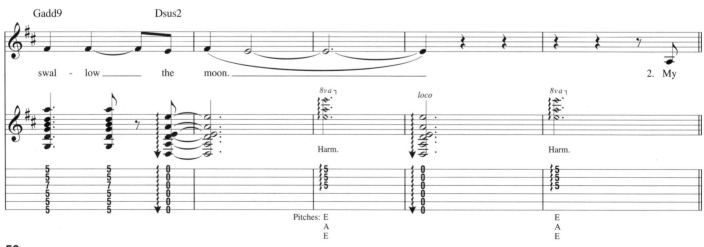

swal - low _____ the moon. _____ 2. My

**Verse**

Gtr. 1: w/ Rhy. Fig. 1 (2 times)

hands are two trav - el - ers, they've crossed o - ceans and lands, ___ yet

*Gtr. 2

Riff A                                                                                       End Riff A

*mf*
*let ring throughout*

*Elec. piano arr. for gtr.
**Symbols in parentheses represent chord names respective to capoed gtrs.
Symbols above reflect actual sounding chords. Capoed fret is "0" in tab.

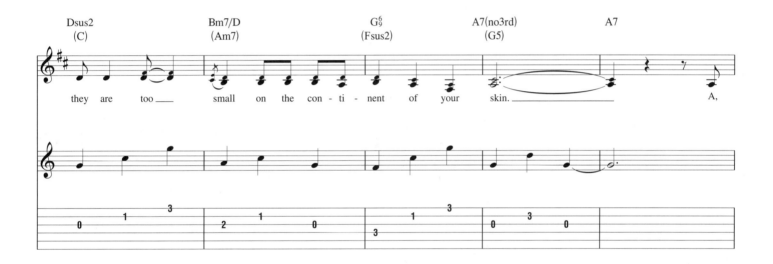

they are too ___ small on the con - ti - nent of your skin. ___ A,

Gtr. 2: w/ Riff A

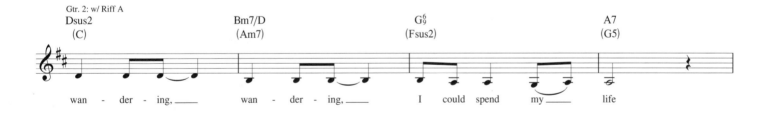

wan - der - ing, ___ wan - der - ing, ___ I could spend my ___ life

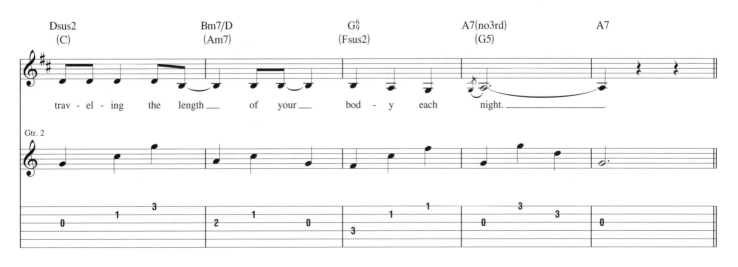

trav - el - ing the length ___ of your ___ bod - y each night. ___

Gtr. 2

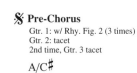

**Pre-Chorus**

Gtr. 1: w/ Rhy. Fig. 2 (3 times)
Gtr. 2: tacet
2nd time, Gtr. 3 tacet

Oh, ____ oh, ____ Ju - pi - ter. ____ Oh, ____ oh,

still my lit - tle heart. ____ Oh, ____ oh, ____ love is a flame,

Gtr. 1: w/ Rhy. Fig. 3

____ nei - ther tim - id ____ nor tame. Take these ____ stars ____

**Chorus**

Gtr. 1: w/ Rhy. Fig. 4

____ from my crown, let the years fall down. ____ Lay me out in fi - re -

light, let my skin feel ____ the night. Fas - ten me to your side, ____ and

say it will be ____ soon. _____ You make me so ____ cra - zy, ba - by, could

*To Coda* ⊕

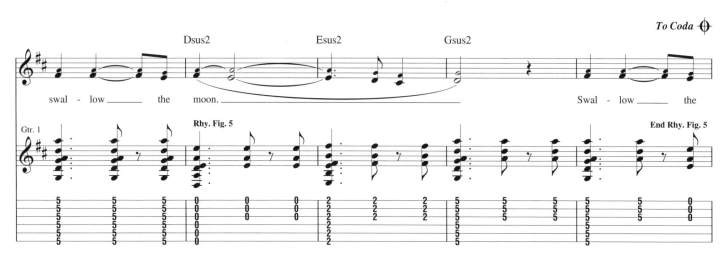

swal - low ____ the moon. _____ Swal - low ____ the

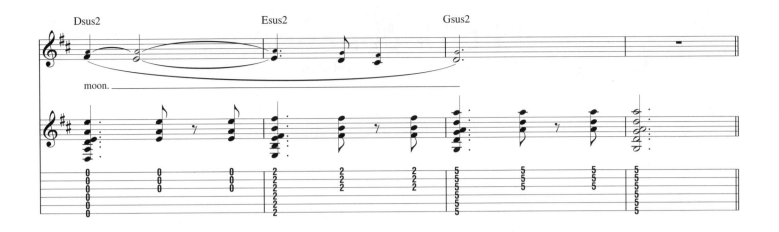

*Piano arr. for gtr.

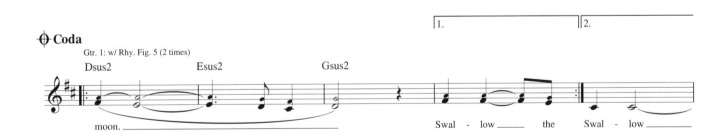

from *Spirit*
# Life Uncommon
**Words and Music by Jewel Kilcher**

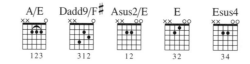

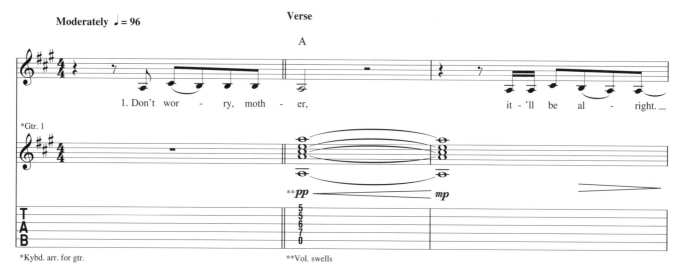

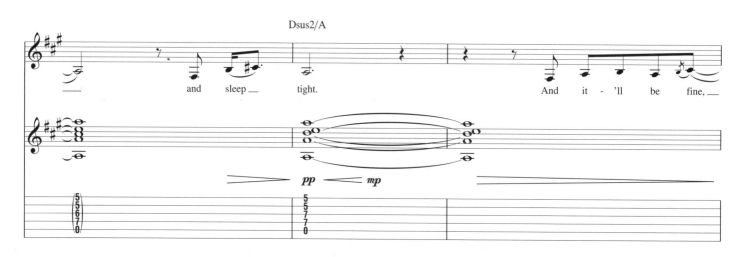

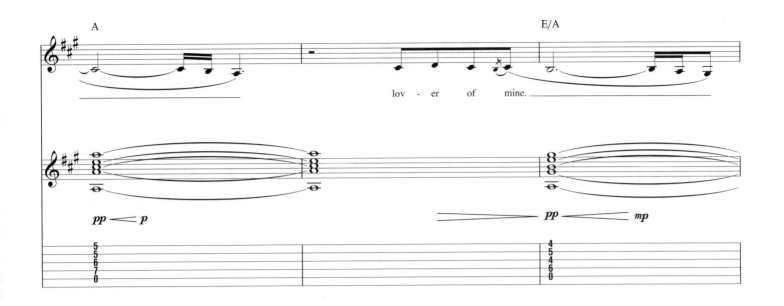

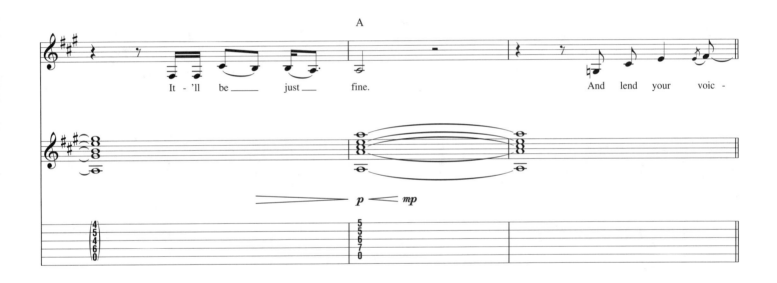

**Chorus**

No long - er lend___ your strength___ to ___ that ___

___ which you wish to be free from. Fill your lives with love and brav - 'ry and you shall lead___

**End Rhy. Fig. 1**

a life___ un - com - mon.___

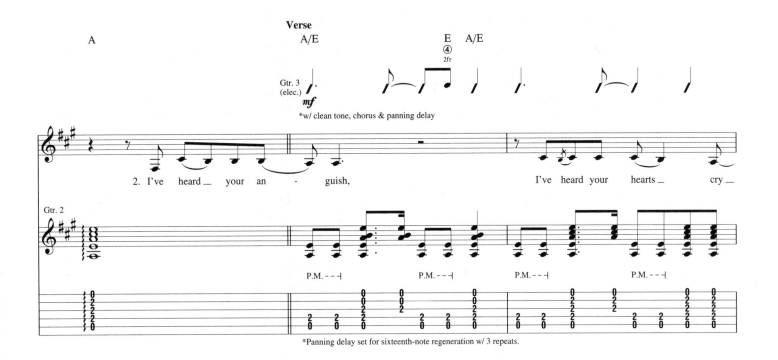

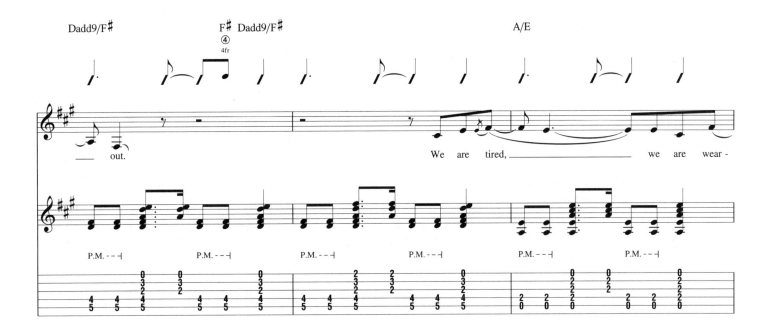

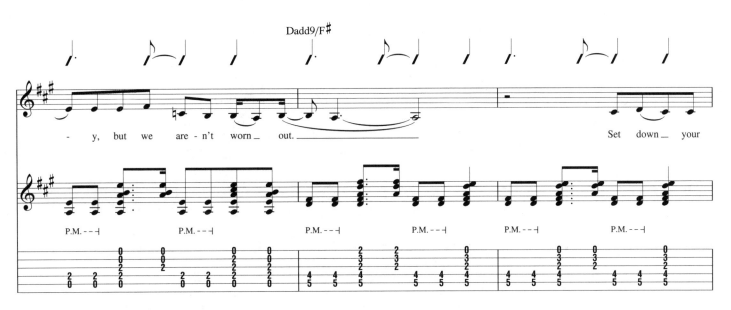

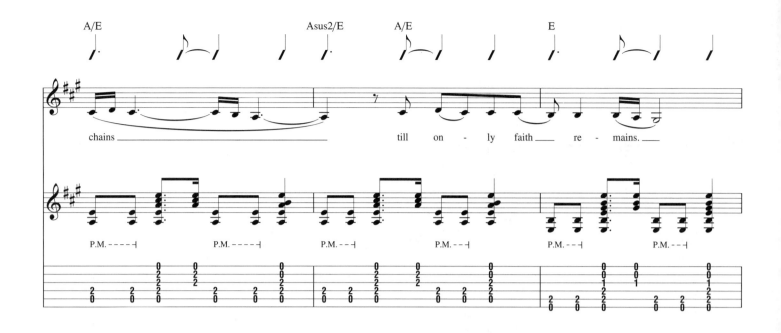

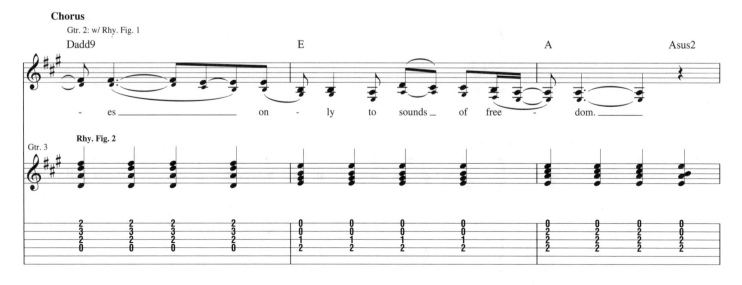

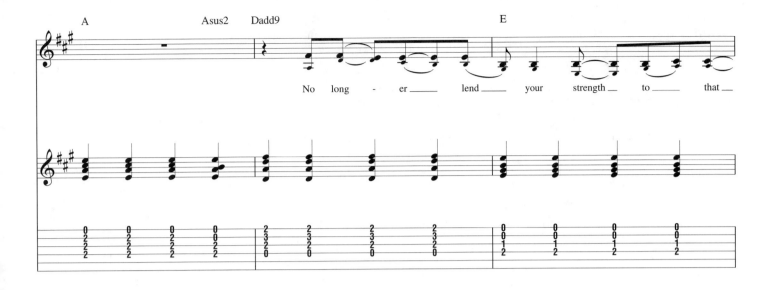

No long - er ___ lend ___ your strength ___ to ___ that ___

___ which you wish to be free from. Fill your lives with love and brav - 'ry and you shall lead ___

**End Rhy. Fig. 2**

(cont. in slashes)

a life ___ un - com - mon. There are

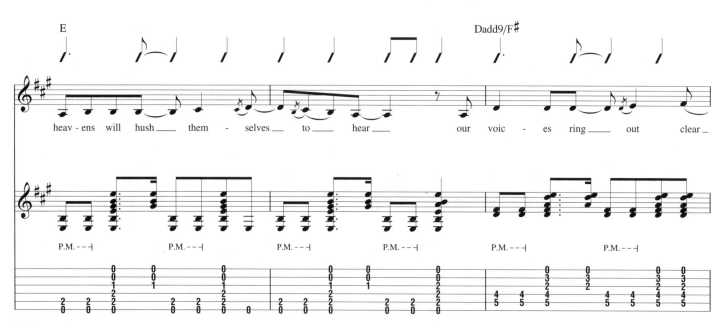

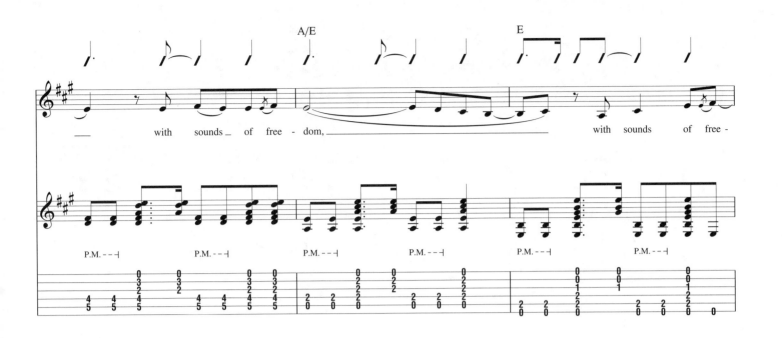

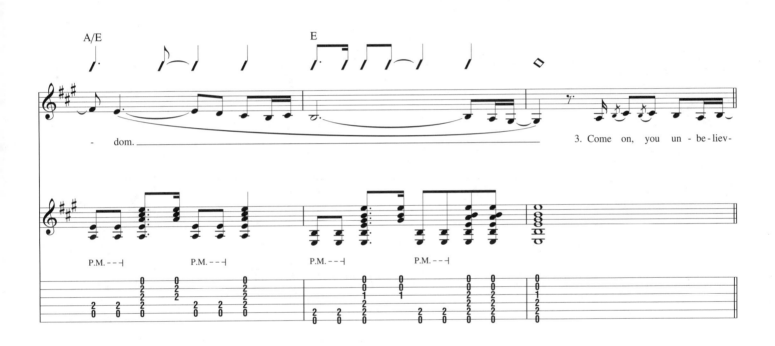

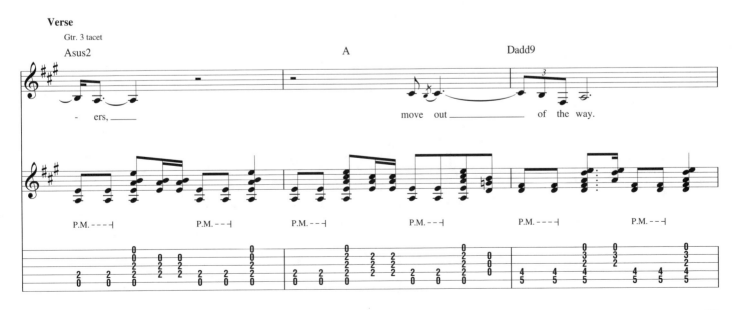

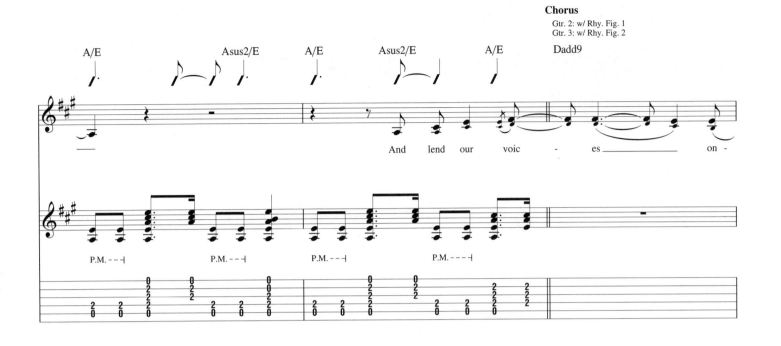

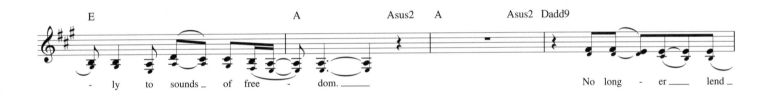

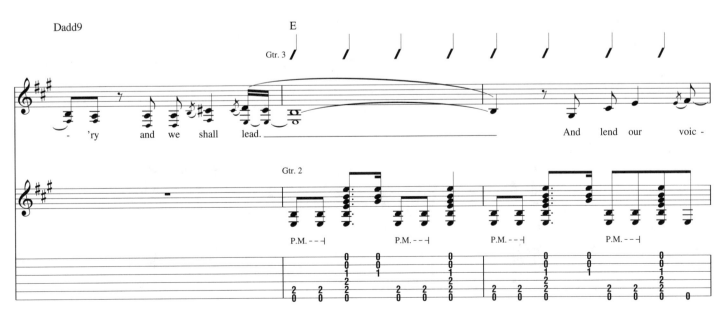

-es ___ on - ly to sounds of free -

dom. ___ No long - er lend ___

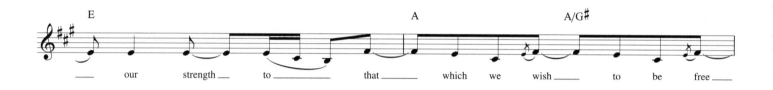

___ our strength ___ to ___ that ___ which we wish ___ to be free ___

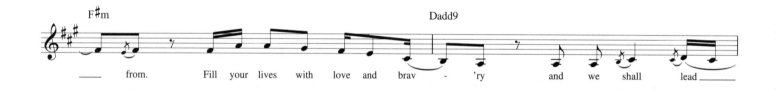

___ from. Fill your lives with love and brav - 'ry and we shall lead ___

a life ___ un - com - mon. ___

# Standing Still

**Words and Music by Rick Nowels and Jewel Kilcher**

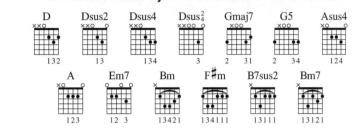

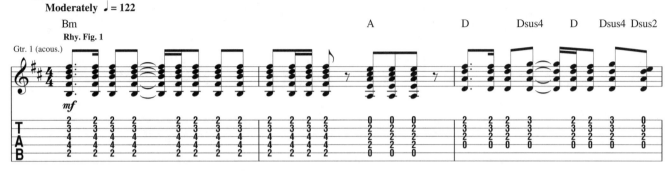

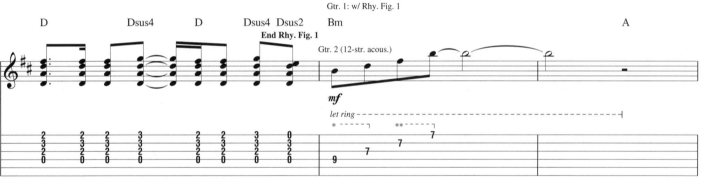

*Pick only the high octave strings.
**Pick only one string each.

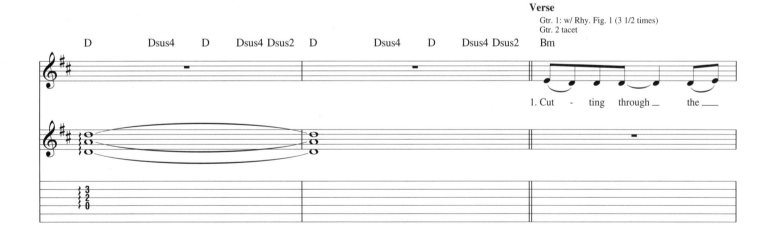

keep __ it clear, __ but I'm los - ing it here __ to the twi - light. __

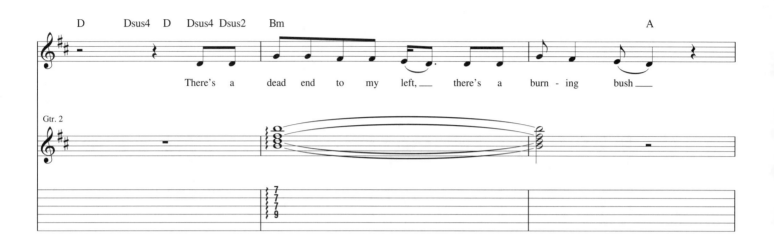

There's a dead end to my left, __ there's a burn - ing bush __

Gtr. 2

*Pick only the high octave strings.

**Pick only one string each.

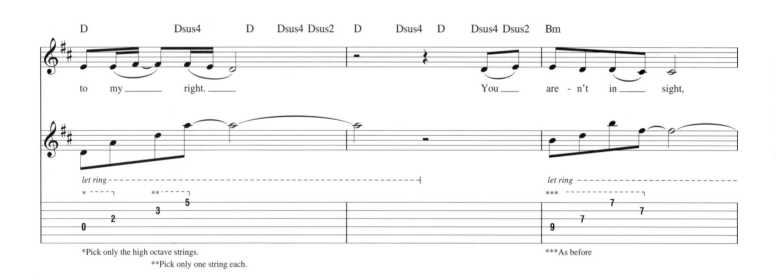

to my __ right. __ You __ are - n't in __ sight,

let ring

***As before

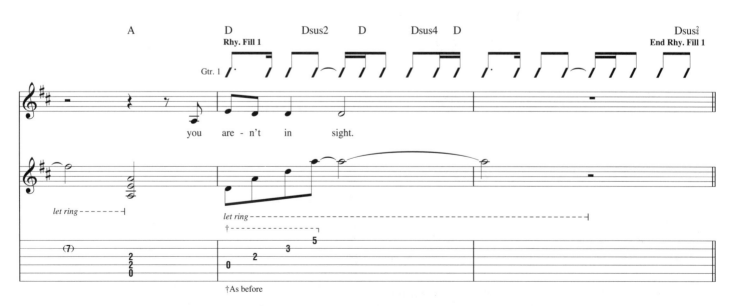

Rhy. Fill 1          End Rhy. Fill 1

Gtr. 1

you are - n't in sight.

let ring

let ring

†As before

**Pre-Chorus**

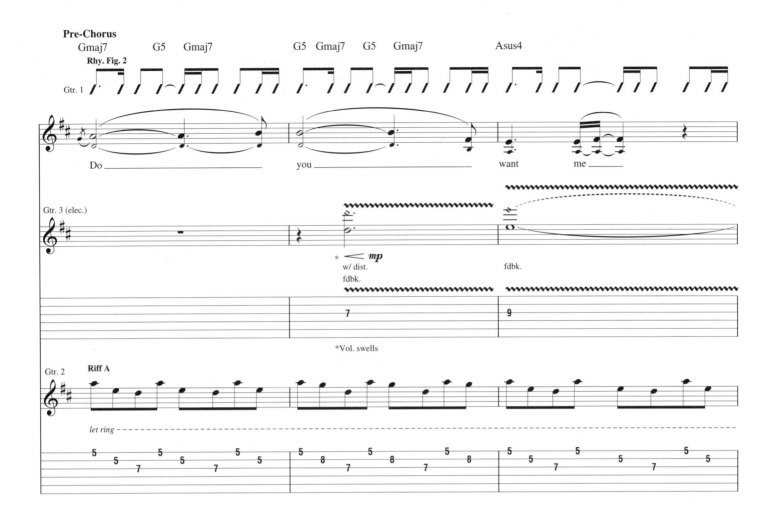

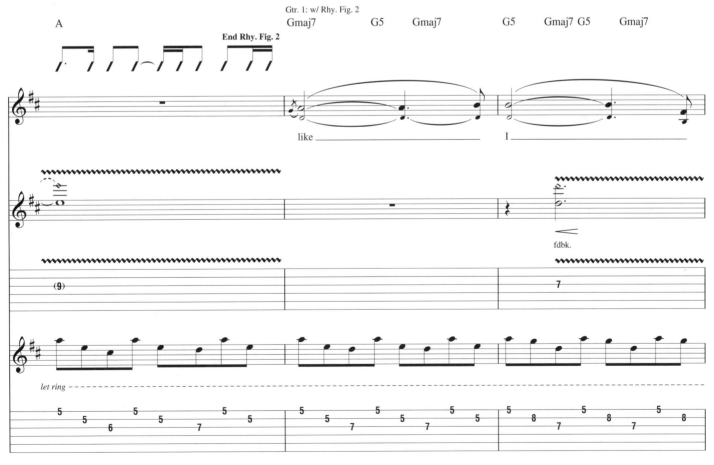

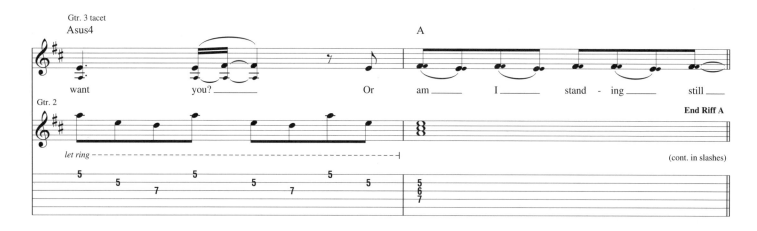

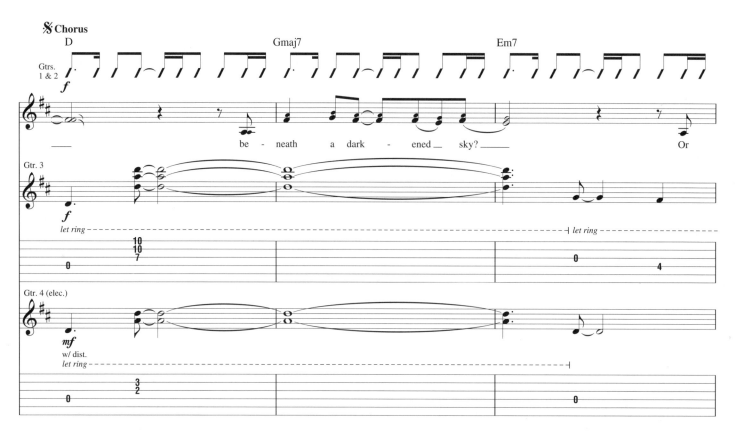

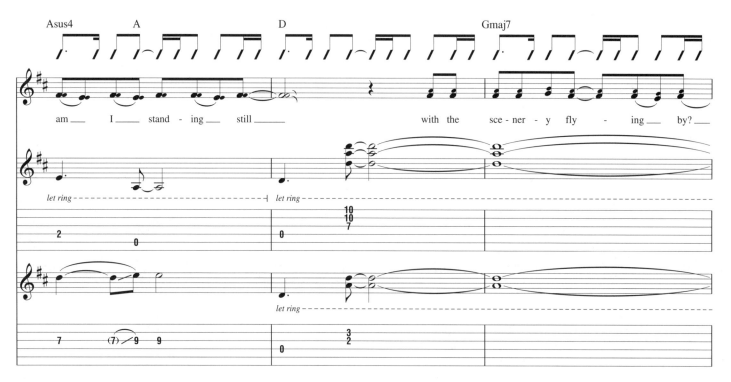

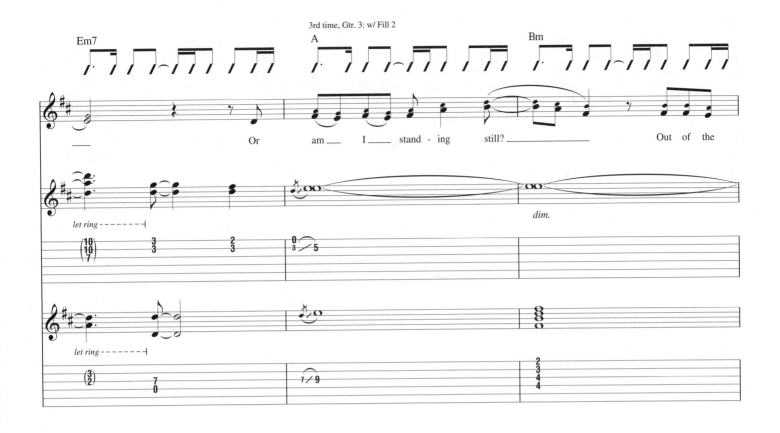

To Coda 1
To Coda 2
2nd & 3rd times, Gtr. 3: w/ Fill 1
F♯m
B7sus2 Bm7 B7sus2 Bm7
Gmaj7
was that you pass - ing me by?
w/ bar
let ring
Asus4
A
let ring
Fill 1
Gtr. 3
let ring

**Verse**

Gtrs. 2 & 3 tacet

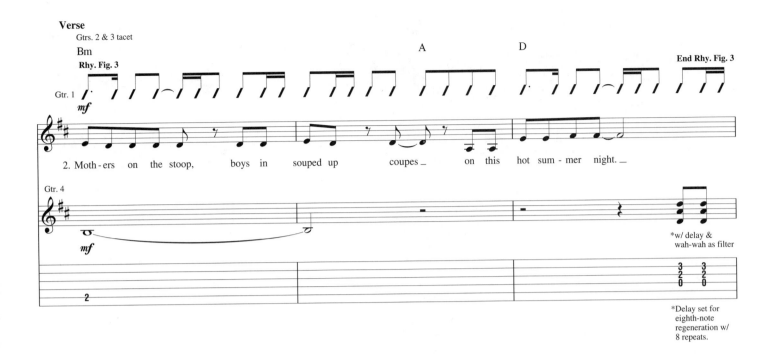

2. Moth - ers on the stoop, boys in souped up coupes _ on this hot sum - mer night. _

*w/ delay &
wah-wah as filter

*Delay set for
eighth-note
regeneration w/
8 repeats.

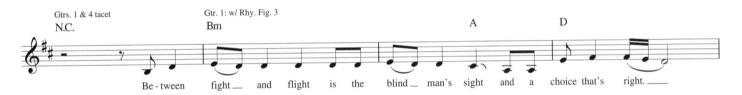

Gtrs. 1 & 4 tacet

Gtr. 1: w/ Rhy. Fig. 3

Be - tween fight _ and flight is the blind _ man's sight and a choice that's right. ____

Gtr. 1: w/ Rhy. Fig. 1 (1 1/2 times)

I roll the win - dow down, feel like I'm, ___ I'm gon - na drown ____ in

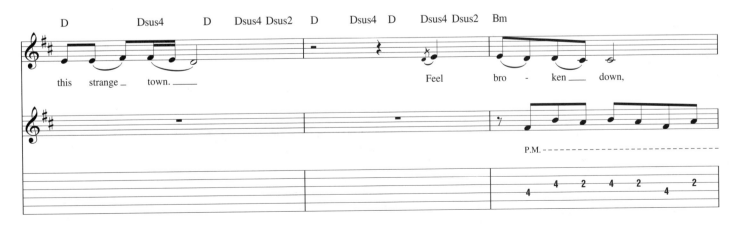

this strange _ town. _____    Feel bro - ken _ down,

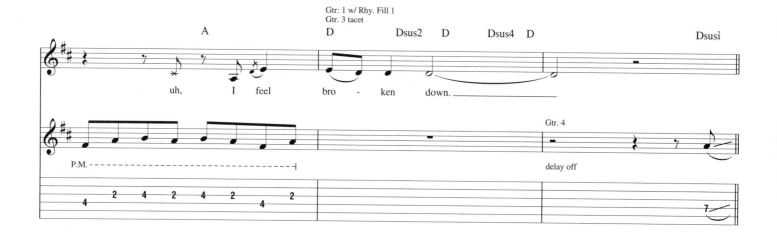

**Pre-Chorus**

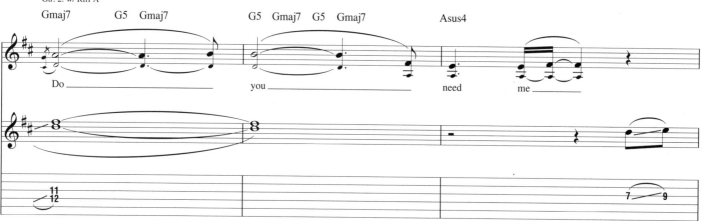

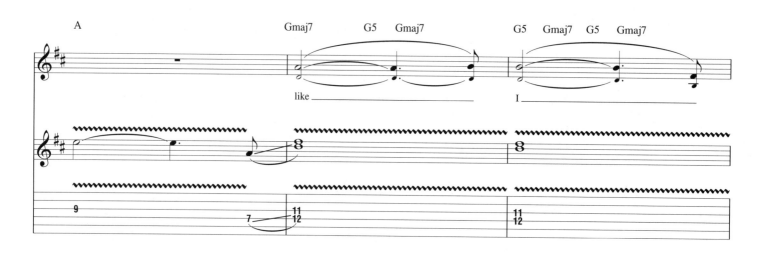

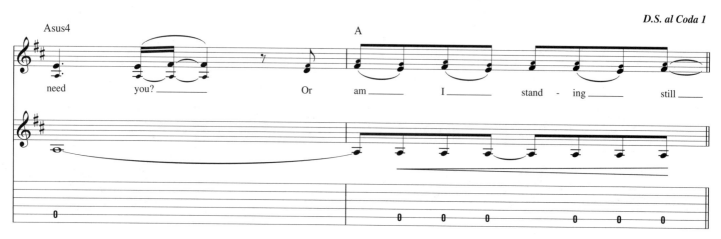

## ⊕ Coda 1

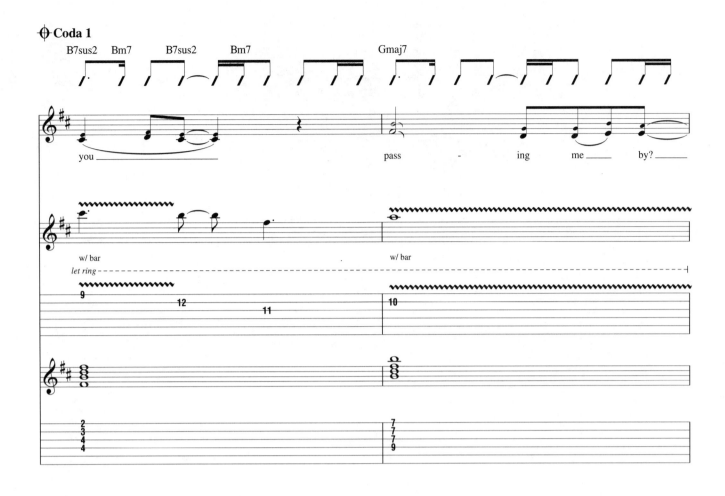

you _____ pass - ing me _____ by? _____

w/ bar

*let ring*

**Bridge**

Gtrs. 1, 2 & 3 tacet

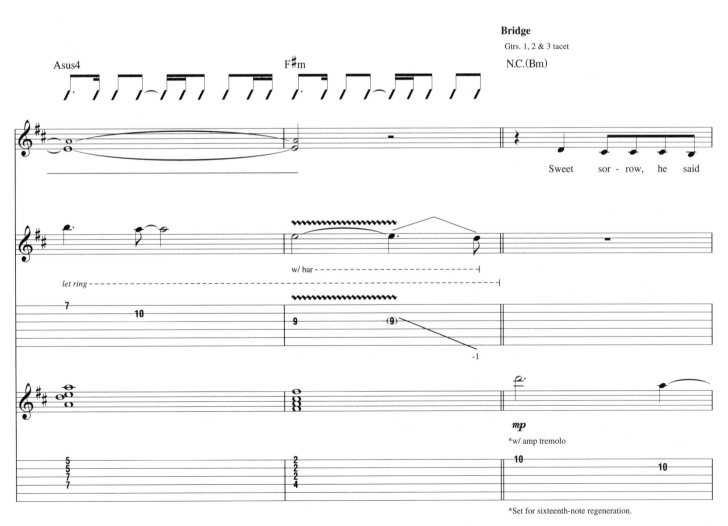

Sweet sor - row, he said

w/ bar

*let ring*

*mp*

*w/ amp tremolo

*Set for sixteenth-note regeneration.

**Interlude**
Gtr. 2: w/ Riff A

*Dsus2

call to-mor-row. Sweet sor-row, he said call to-mor-row. Do _____

Gtr. 4

dim.

*Chord symbols reflect implied harmony.

Gtr. 4 tacet
Gsus2                Asus4              A    Asus4    Dsus2

you _____ love me _____ like _____

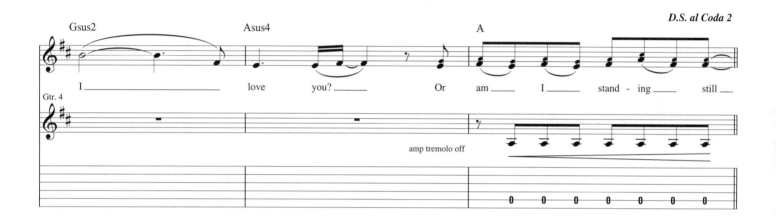

*D.S. al Coda 2*

Gsus2                Asus4                        A

I _____ love you? _____ Or am ___ I ___ stand-ing ___ still ___

Gtr. 4

amp tremolo off

**Coda 2**

B7sus2  Bm7  B7sus2  Bm7                Gmaj7

you                    pass - ing me ___ by? _____

w/ bar
*let ring* - - - - - - - - - - - - - - - - - -

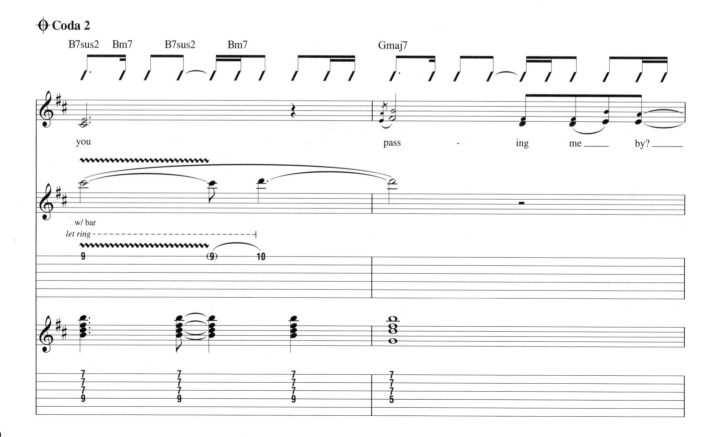

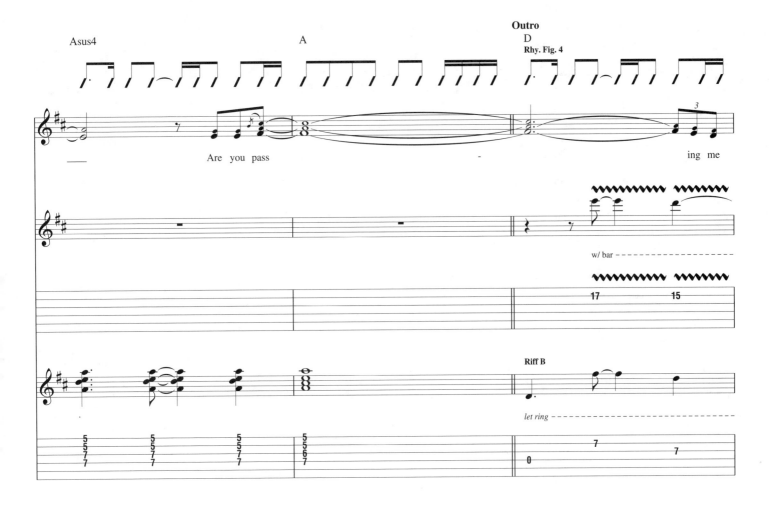

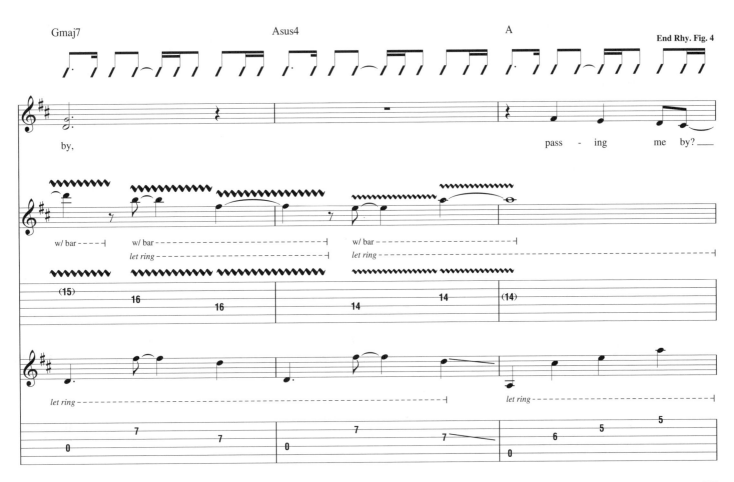

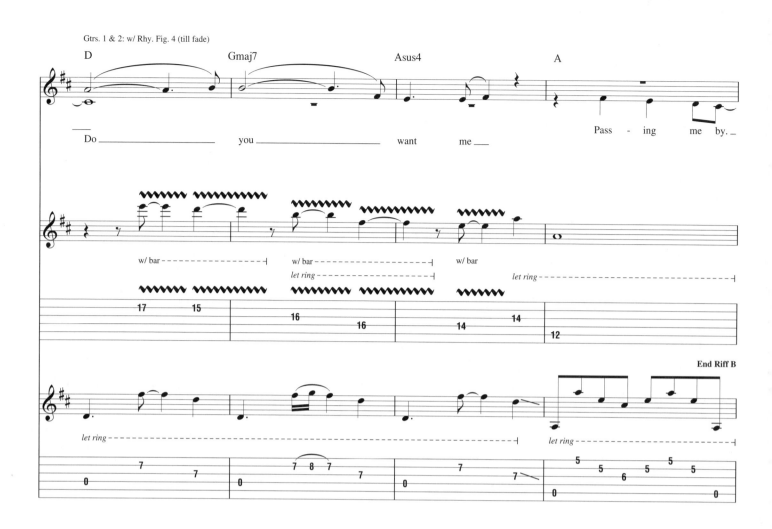

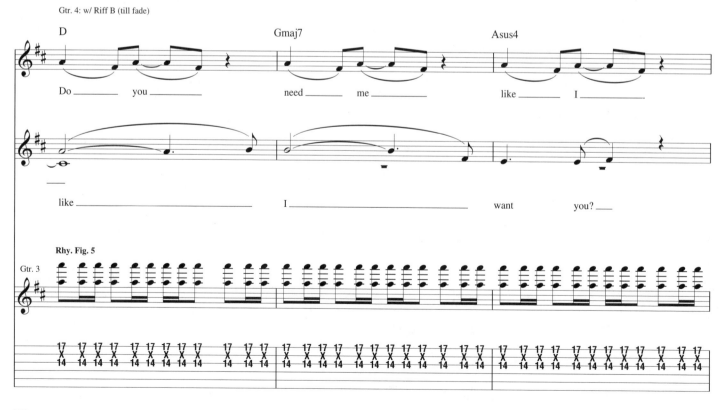

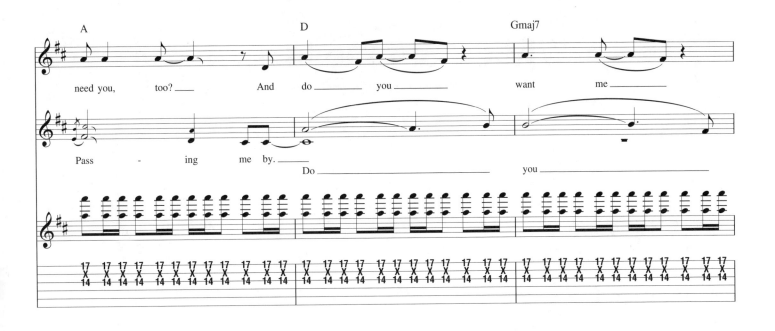

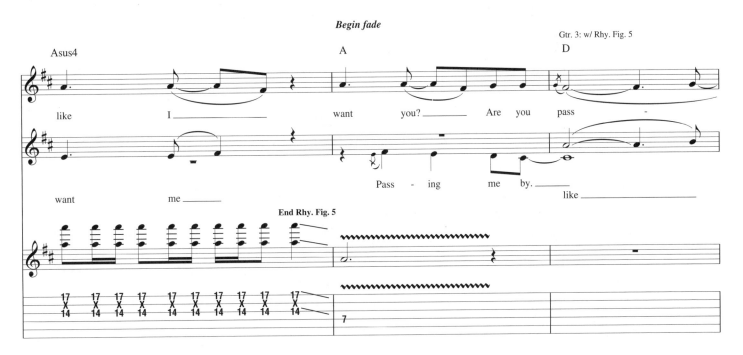

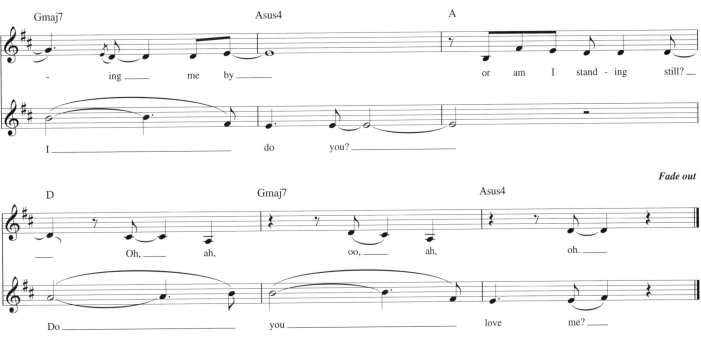

from *Spirit*

# What's Simple Is True

### Words and Music by Jewel Kilcher

Gtr. 1: Capo II

**Intro**
**Moderately slow** ♩. = 44

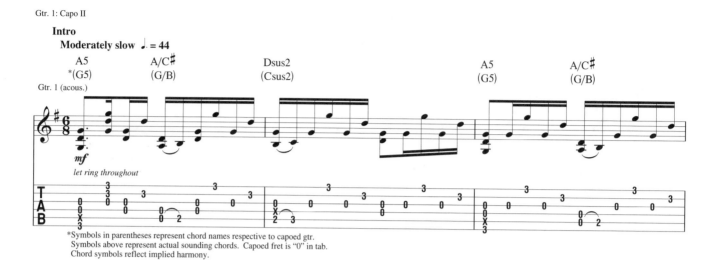

*Symbols in parentheses represent chord names respective to capoed gtr.
Symbols above represent actual sounding chords. Capoed fret is "0" in tab.
Chord symbols reflect implied harmony.

**Verse**

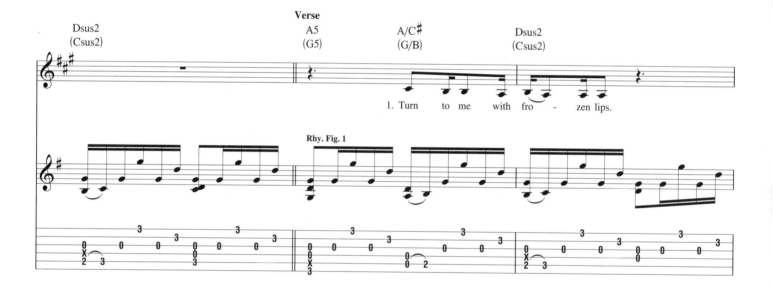

1. Turn to me with fro - zen lips.

Your hands are ic - y cold. ___ Your eyes burn ___ bright a - gainst the

frost - bit sky. _____ You nev - er seemed more love - ly than you

do _____ to - night. _____

**Verse**

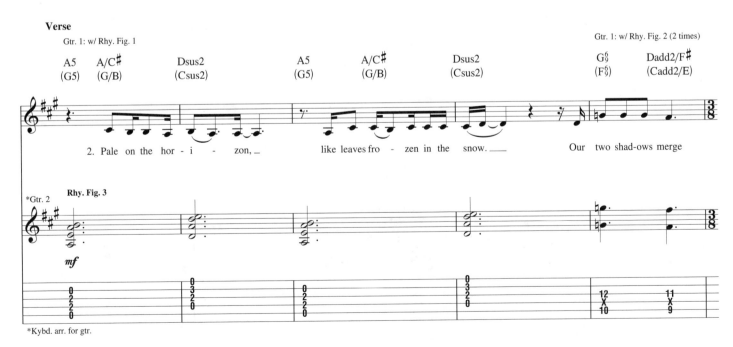

2. Pale on the hor - i - zon, _ like leaves fro - zen in the snow. _ Our two shad-ows merge

*Kybd. arr. for gtr.

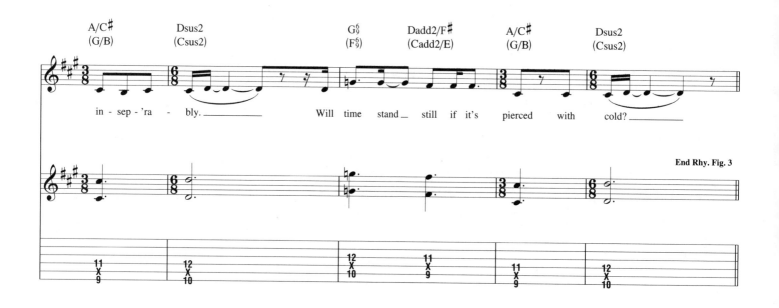

in - sep - 'ra - bly. _____ Will time stand _ still if it's pierced with cold? _____

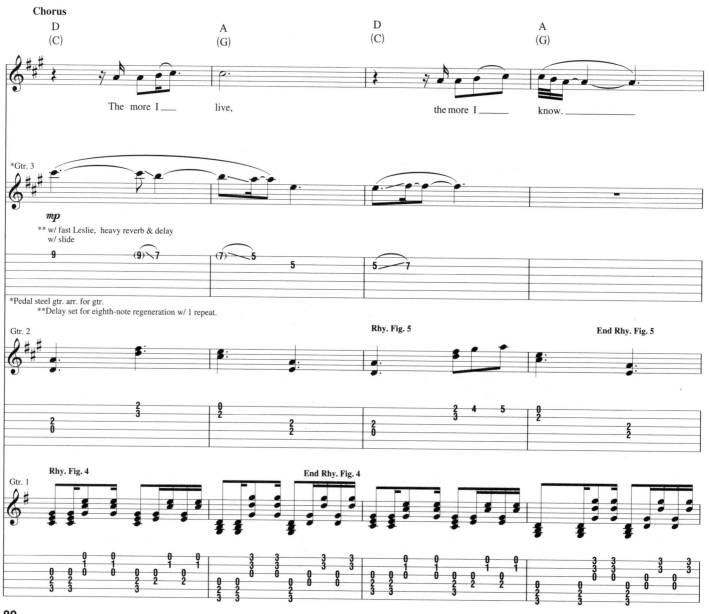

**Chorus**

The more I ___ live, the more I ___ know. _____

*Gtr. 3

*Pedal steel gtr. arr. for gtr.
**Delay set for eighth-note regeneration w/ 1 repeat.

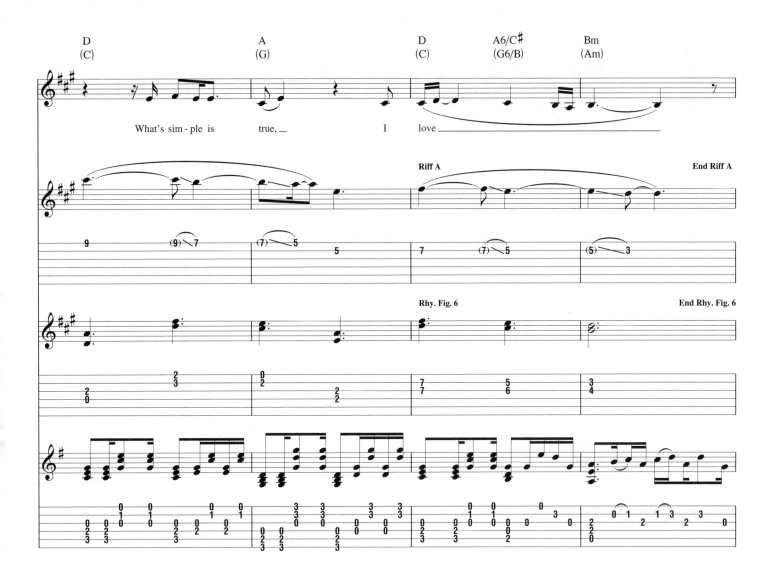

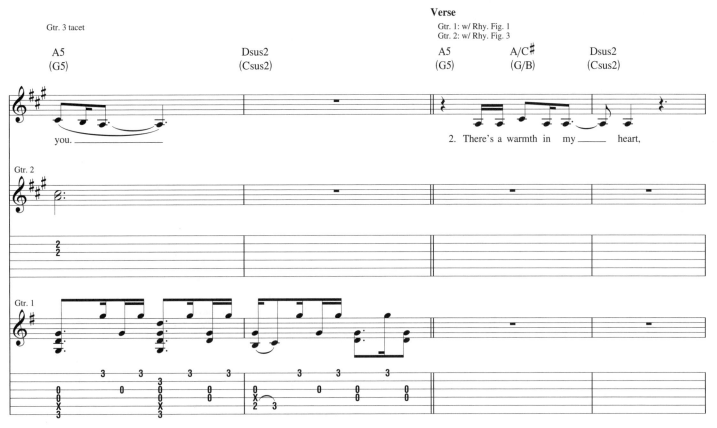

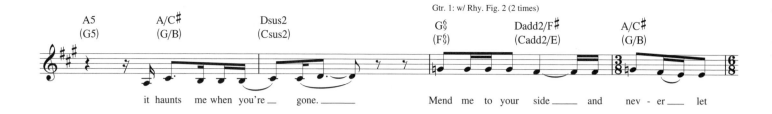

it haunts me when you're __ gone. _____ Mend me to your side _____ and nev - er __ let

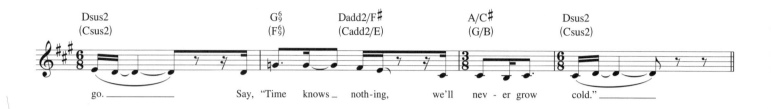

go. _____ Say, "Time knows __ noth-ing, we'll nev - er grow cold." ____

**Chorus**

Gtr. 1: w/ Rhy. Fig. 4 (3 times)
Gtr. 2: w/ Rhy. Fig. 5 (3 times)

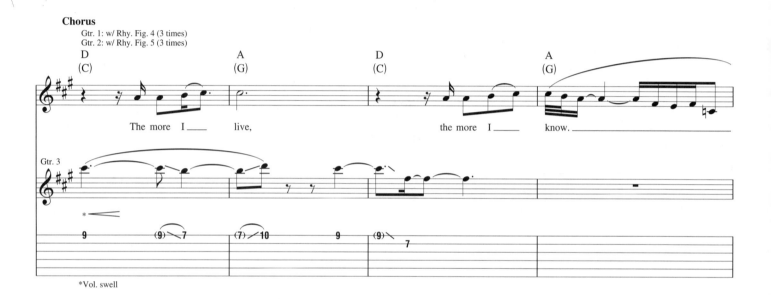

The more I ____ live, the more I ____ know. _____

*Vol. swell

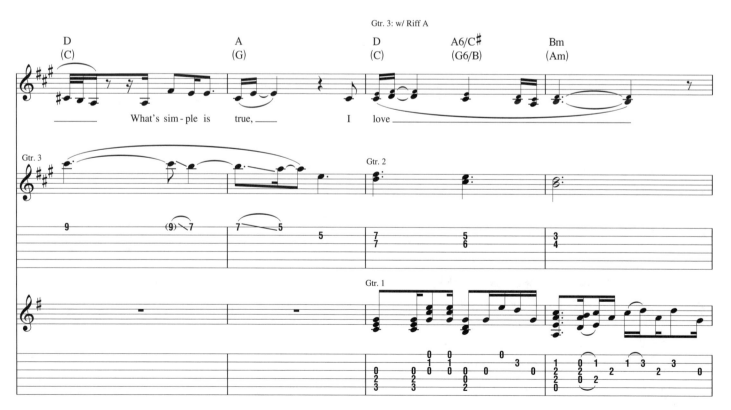

What's sim - ple is true, ____ I love _____

**Bridge**

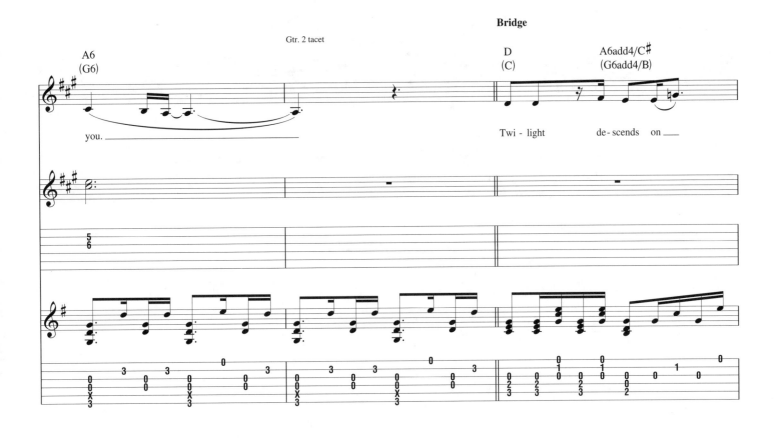

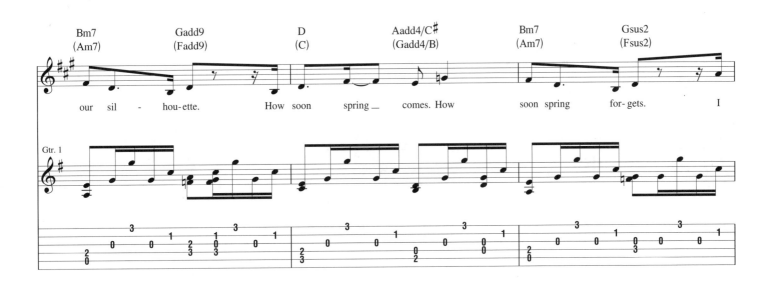

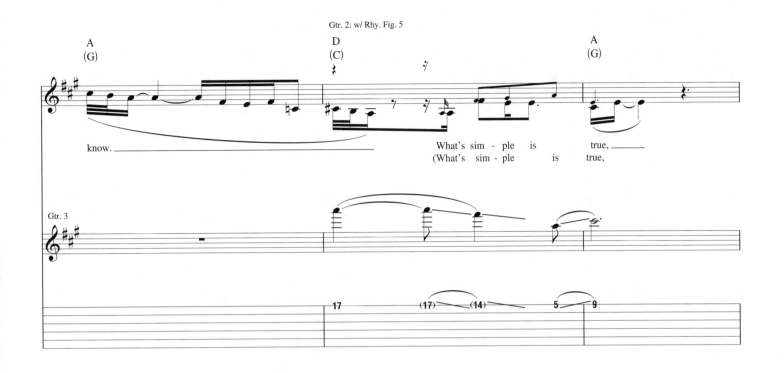

Gtr. 2: w/ Rhy. Fig. 5

know. _____ What's sim - ple is true, _____
(What's sim - ple is true,

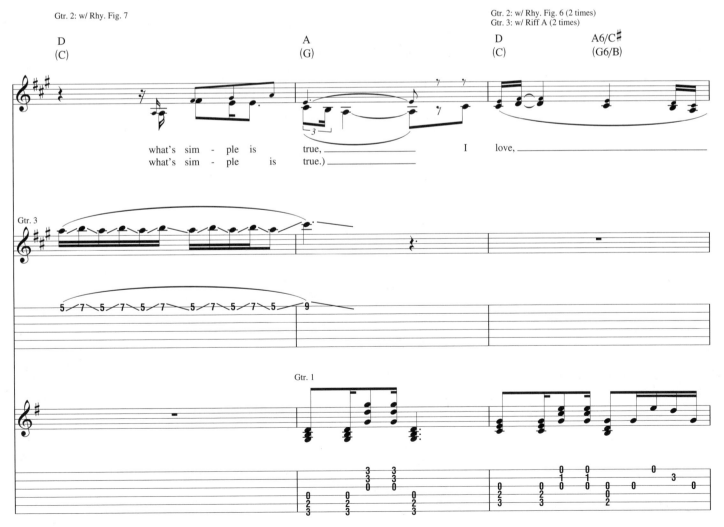

Gtr. 2: w/ Rhy. Fig. 7

Gtr. 2: w/ Rhy. Fig. 6 (2 times)
Gtr. 3: w/ Riff A (2 times)

what's sim - ple is true, _____ I love, _____
what's sim - ple is true.) _____

# Who Will Save Your Soul

## Words and Music by Jewel Kilcher

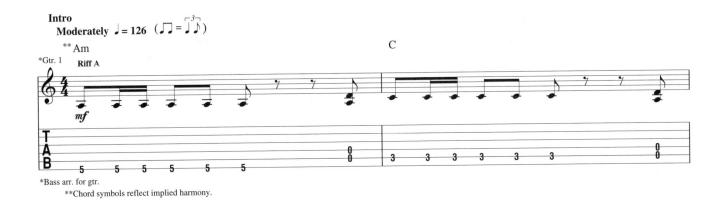

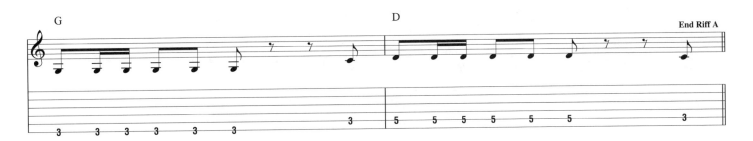

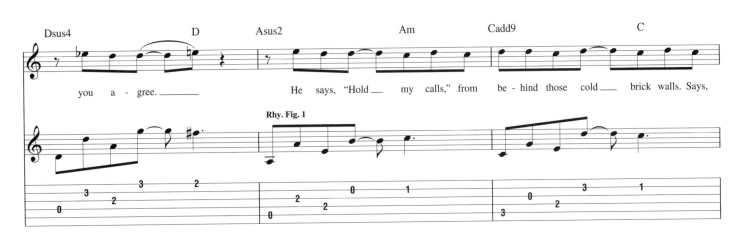

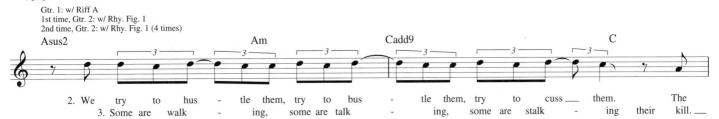

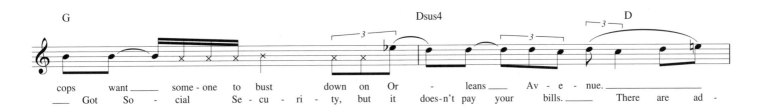

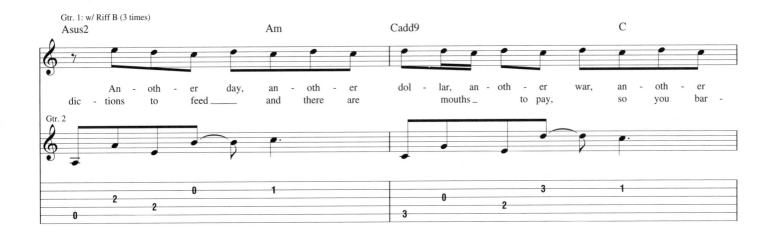

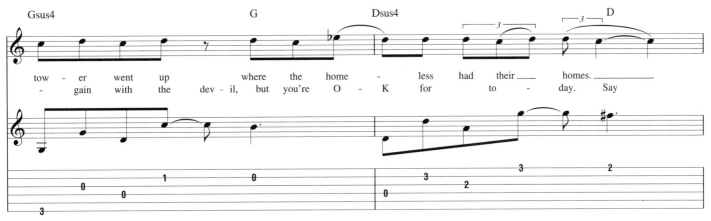

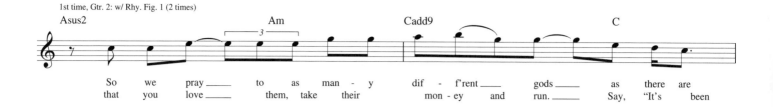

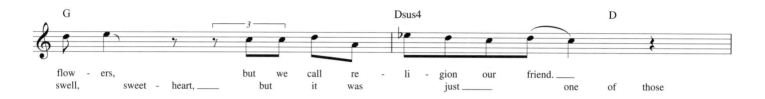

So we pray ___ to as man - y dif - f'rent ___ gods ___ as there are
that you love ___ them, take their mon - ey and run. ___ Say, "It's been

flow - ers, but we call re - li - gion our friend. ___
swell, sweet - heart, ___ but it was just ___ one of those

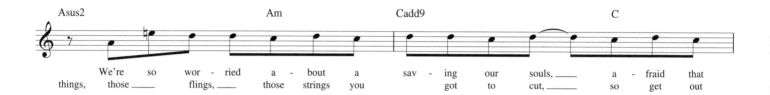

We're so wor - ried a - bout a sav - ing our souls, ___ a - fraid that
things, those ___ flings, ___ those strings you got to cut, ___ so get out

*To Coda 2* ⊕        *D.S. al Coda 1*

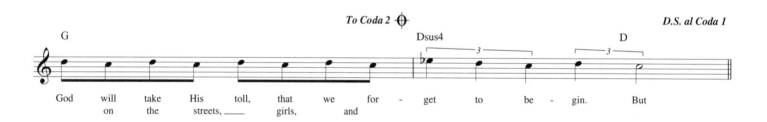

God will take His toll, that we for - get to be - gin. But
on the streets, ___ girls, and

⊕ **Coda 1**

La, da, da, da, ___ di, da, da, da, da, da, ya, ___ di. ___

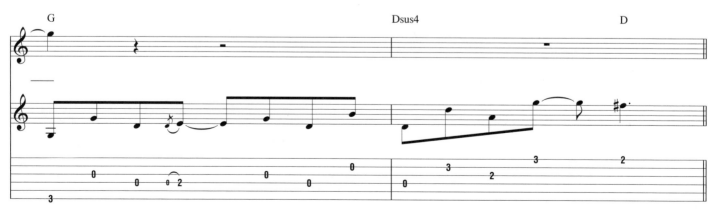

90

**Interlude**

Gtr. 2 tacet

N.C.(Em)

*D.S.S. al Coda 2*

⊕ **Coda 2**

**Outro**

Gtr. 1: w/ Riff B (till fade)
Gtr. 2: w/ Rhy. Fig. 1 (till fade)

| Dsus4 | D | Asus2 | Am | Cadd9 | C |
|---|---|---|---|---|---|

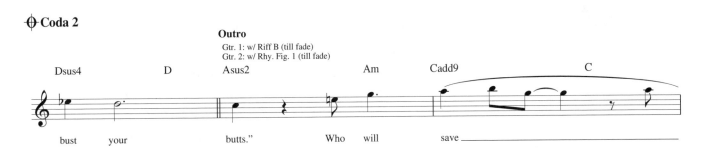

bust      your      butts."      Who      will      save

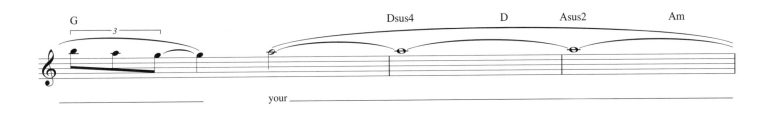

your

soul?      Ba - by,   come,   lit - tle   ba - by,   yeah.

*Repeat and fade*

w/ Lead Voc. ad lib. (till fade)

| Asus2 | Am | Cadd9 | C | G | Dsus4 | D |
|---|---|---|---|---|---|---|

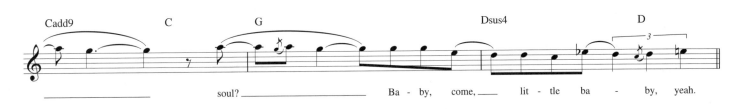

from *Pieces of You*

# You Were Meant for Me

### Words and Music by Jewel Kilcher and Steve Poltz

Gtr. 1: w/ Riff A, simile

I break the yolks and make a smile - y face. I kind - a like it in my

brand - new place. Wipe the spots off of the mirror, don't leave my keys in the door. I

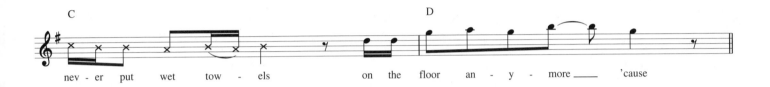

nev - er put wet tow - els on the floor an - y - more 'cause

**Chorus**

dreams last so long, e - ven af - ter you're gone.

I know that you love me and soon you will see you were

* slight vibrato

*Additional Lyrics*

2. I called my momma, she was out for a walk.
Consoled a cup of coffee but it didn't wanna talk.
So I picked up the paper, it was more bad news;
More hearts being broken or people being used.
Put on my coat in the pouring rain.
I saw a movie, it just wasn't the same
'Cause it was happy, oh, I was sad
And it made me miss you, oh, so bad 'cause...

3. I brush my teeth, I put the cap back on.
I know you hate it when I leave the light on.
I pick a book up and then I turn the sheets down
And then I take a deep breath and a good look around.
Put on my PJs and hop into bed.
I'm half alive but I feel mostly dead.
I try and tell myself it'll all be alright.
I just shouldn't think anymore tonight 'cause...

# Guitar Notation Legend

Guitar Music can be notated three different ways: on a *musical staff*, in *tablature*, and in *rhythm slashes*.

**RHYTHM SLASHES** are written above the staff. Strum chords in the rhythm indicated. Use the chord diagrams found at the top of the first page of the transcription for the appropriate chord voicings. Round noteheads indicate single notes.

**THE MUSICAL STAFF** shows pitches and rhythms and is divided by bar lines into measures. Pitches are named after the first seven letters of the alphabet.

**TABLATURE** graphically represents the guitar fingerboard. Each horizontal line represents a string, and each number represents a fret.

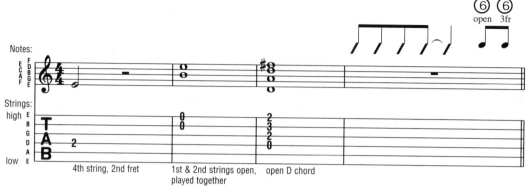

4th string, 2nd fret    1st & 2nd strings open, played together    open D chord

**HALF-STEP BEND:** Strike the note and bend up 1/2 step.

**WHOLE-STEP BEND:** Strike the note and bend up one step.

**GRACE NOTE BEND:** Strike the note and immediately bend up as indicated.

**SLIGHT (MICROTONE) BEND:** Strike the note and bend up 1/4 step.

**BEND AND RELEASE:** Strike the note and bend up as indicated, then release back to the original note. Only the first note is struck.

**PRE-BEND:** Bend the note as indicated, then strike it.

**VIBRATO:** The string is vibrated by rapidly bending and releasing the note with the fretting hand.

**WIDE VIBRATO:** The pitch is varied to a greater degree by vibrating with the fretting hand.

**HAMMER-ON:** Strike the first (lower) note with one finger, then sound the higher note (on the same string) with another finger by fretting it without picking.

**PULL-OFF:** Place both fingers on the notes to be sounded. Strike the first note and without picking, pull the finger off to sound the second (lower) note.

**LEGATO SLIDE:** Strike the first note and then slide the same fret-hand finger up or down to the second note. The second note is not struck.

**SHIFT SLIDE:** Same as legato slide, except the second note is struck.

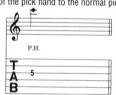

**TRILL:** Very rapidly alternate between the notes indicated by continuously hammering on and pulling off.

**TAPPING:** Hammer ("tap") the fret indicated with the pick-hand index or middle finger and pull off to the note fretted by the fret hand.

**NATURAL HARMONIC:** Strike the note while the fret-hand lightly touches the string directly over the fret indicated.

**PINCH HARMONIC:** The note is fretted normally and a harmonic is produced by adding the edge of the thumb or the tip of the index finger of the pick hand to the normal pick attack.

**PICK SCRAPE:** The edge of the pick is rubbed down (or up) the string, producing a scratchy sound.

**MUFFLED STRINGS:** A percussive sound is produced by laying the fret hand across the string(s) without depressing, and striking them with the pick hand.

**PALM MUTING:** The note is partially muted by the pick hand lightly touching the string(s) just before the bridge.

**RAKE:** Drag the pick across the strings indicated with a single motion.

**TREMOLO PICKING:** The note is picked as rapidly and continuously as possible.

**VIBRATO BAR DIVE AND RETURN:** The pitch of the note or chord is dropped a specified number of steps (in rhythm) then returned to the original pitch.

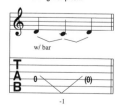

**VIBRATO BAR SCOOP:** Depress the bar just before striking the note, then quickly release the bar.

**VIBRATO BAR DIP:** Strike the note and then immediately drop a specified number of steps, then release back to the original pitch.